Illustrated

Bicycle Trails

of

Iowa

D0109801

An American Bike Trails Publication

Bicycle Trails of Iowa

Published by   American Bike Trails
1157 South Milwaukee Avenue
Libertyville, IL   60048

Photo: By Bill Burnes
Courtesy of Iowa Dept. of Transportation

Created by   Ray Hoven
Designed by   Mary C. Rumpsa

Introduction

Table of Contents

Central Iowa

Western Iowa

Appendices & Indexes

The Iowa Trails Council

The Iowa Trails Council (ITC) is pleased to have participated in the creation of this book. It is our hope that you will find it helpful and that it will provide many days of enjoyment on Iowa's trails.

The Council was founded in 1984. Its purpose is to acquire land for trails, to help develop trails and promote them when completed. It is the only organization in Iowa devoted exclusively to this cause.

The ITC is a not-for-profit membership organization. Its officers and staff are all volunteers working to create more and better trails in Iowa. The ITC publishes a mini-magazine which is distributed to its members in an effort to keep them informed of new and extended trails both inside and outside Iowa, as well as attractions near these trails.

The Council has, since its founding, specialized in acquiring former railroad rights-of-way for conversion to trails. Until very recently Iowa has led the nation in both the number of these rail beds converted and the total mileage, which now amounts to more than 650 miles on 50 former rail corridors. Iowa has consistently maintained its average of approximately 10 percent of the nation's rail-trail conversions.

More often than not these conversions are referred to as bike trails, though they are designed to be multi-purpose. More and more of these are being hard surfaced to satisfy bicyclists and in-line skaters. The ITC initiated the effort to bring the nation's longest trail, coast to coast from California to Delaware, on a 500 mile route across Iowa. Bicyclists are obviously the chief benefactors of the efforts of the Council.

Sandwiched between two of the nation's major rivers, Iowa offers a surprising variety of seasons. The state's rolling terrain can provide both leisurely rides and real outdoor adventure. Many delightful trails can be found in Iowa's state and county parks while other trails act as connectors of these parks or link together metropolitan areas. There are many and various attractions along the way to satisfy most any interest, from museums to covered bridges, from casinos to racing tracks, from fall festivals to movie making sites. No matter where you go we believe you will find friendly faces and the welcome mat will always be out.

New members of the Iowa Trails Council are also most welcome, whether they live inside or outside Iowa. Information may be obtained by writing to the Iowa Trails Council, Post Office Box 131, Center Point, IA, 52213-0131 or by telephoning (319) 849-1844.

Tom F. Neenan

ITC Executive Director

How To Use This Book

This book provides a comprehensive, easy-to-use quick reference to the many off-road trails throughout Iowa. It contains over 85 detailed trail maps, plus overviews covering the state sectionally, organized by east, central and west. Trails are listed alphabetically within each section. The sectional overviews are grouped near the front, with a section cross-referencing counties and towns to trails, and a section listing many of the parks in Iowa with their pertinent information. Each trail map includes such helpful features as location and access, trail facilities, nearby communities and their populations.

Terms Used

Length	Expressed in miles. Round trip mileage is normally indicated for loops.
Effort Levels	*Easy* Physical exertion is not strenuous. Climbs and descents as well as technical obstacles are more minimal. Recommended for beginners.
	Moderate Physical exertion is not excessive. Climbs and descents can be challenging. Expect some technical obstacles.
	Difficult Physical exertion is demanding. Climbs and descents require good riding skills. Trail surface may be sandy, loose rock, soft or wet.
Directions	Describes by way of directions and distances, how to get to the trail areas from roads and nearby communities.
Map	Illustrative representation of a geographic area, such as a state, section, forest, park or trail complex.
Forest	Typically encompasses a dense growth of trees and underbrush covering a large tract.
Park	A tract of land generally including woodlands and open areas.
DNR	Department of Natural Resources

Types of Biking

Mountain	Fat-tired bikes are recommended. Ride may be generally flat but then with a soft, rocky or wet surface.
Leisure	Off-road gentle ride. Surface is generally paved or screened.
Tour	Riding on roads with motorized traffic or on road shoulders.

Riding Tips

- Pushing in gears that are too high can push knees beyond their limits. Avoid extremes by pedaling faster rather than shifting into a higher gear.

- Keeping your elbows bent, changing your hand position frequently and wearing bicycle gloves all help to reduce the numbness or pain in the palm of the hand from long-distance riding.

- Keep you pedal rpms up on an uphill so you have reserve power if you lose speed.

- Stay in a high-gear on a level surface, placing pressure on the pedals and resting on the handle bars and saddle.

- Lower your center of gravity on a long or steep downhill run by using the quick release seat post binder and dropping the saddle height down.

- Brake intermittently on a rough surface.

- Wear proper equipment. Wear a helmet that is approved by the Snell Memorial Foundation or the American National Standards Institute. Look for one of their stickers inside the helmet.

- Use a lower tire inflation pressure for riding on unpaved surfaces. The lower pressure will provide better tire traction and a more comfortable ride.

- Apply your brakes gradually to maintain control on loose gravel or soil.

- Ride only on trails designated for bicycles or in areas where you have the permission of the landowner.

- Be courteous to hikers or horseback riders on the trail, they have the right of way.

- Leave riding trails in the condition you found them. Be sensitive to the environment. Properly dispose of your trash. If you open a gate, close it behind you.

- Don't carry items or attach anything to your bicycle that might hinder your vision or control.

- Don't wear anything that restricts your hearing.

- Don't carry extra clothing where it can hang down and jam in a wheel.

Explanation of Symbols

ROUTES

━━━━━━ Biking Trail
▬▬▬▬ Bikeway
▬ ▬ ▬ ▬ Alternate Bike Trail
▪▬▪▬▪▬ Undeveloped Trail
■ ■ ■ ■ Alternate Use Trail
= = = = Planned Trail
━━━━━━ Roadway

FACILITIES

🔧 Bike Repair
🅰 Camping
➕ First Aid
❓ Info
🛏 Lodging
🅿 Parking
🎪 Picnic
🍺 Refreshments
🚻 Restrooms
🏠 Shelter
🚰 Water
MF Multi Facilities Available

Refreshments	First Aid
Telephone	Picnic
Restrooms	Lodging

TRAIL USES

 Mountain Biking

 Leisure Biking

 In Line Skating

 (X-C) Cross-Country Skiing

 Hiking

🐎 Horseback Riding

🛷 Snowmobiling

ROAD RELATED SYMBOLS

(45) Interstate Highway
(45) U.S. Highway
(45) State Highway
45 County Highway

AREA DESCRIPTIONS

▪ Parks, Schools, Preserves, etc.
▪ Waterway
▬ Mileage Scale
 Directional

State of Iowa

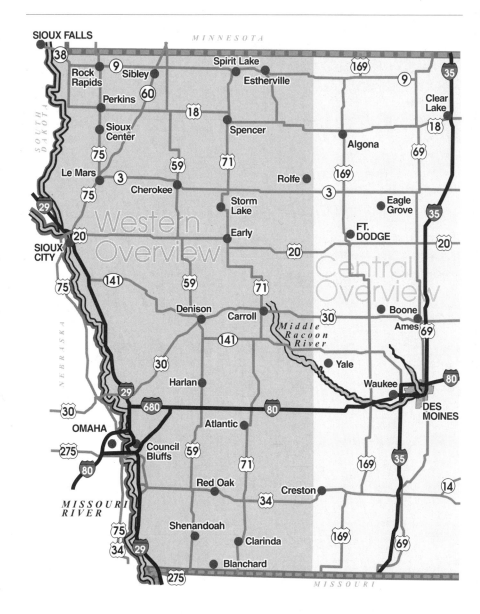

Shaded Relief Map
of the Topographic Surface of Iowa

Courtesy of Iowa Dept. of Transportation

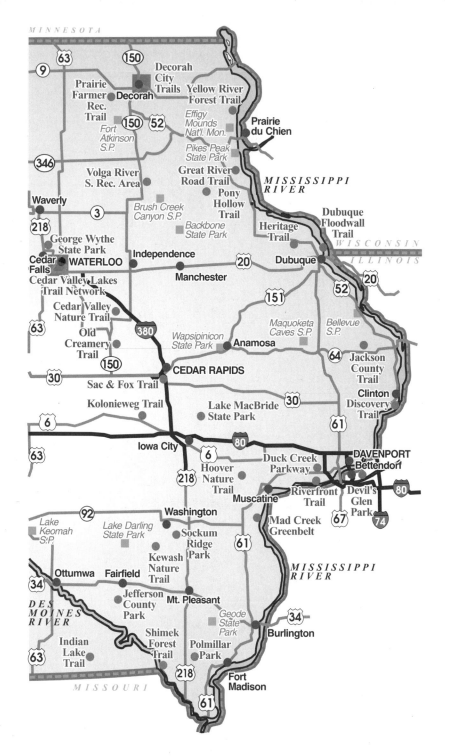

Eastern Iowa Overview

Eastern Iowa Trails

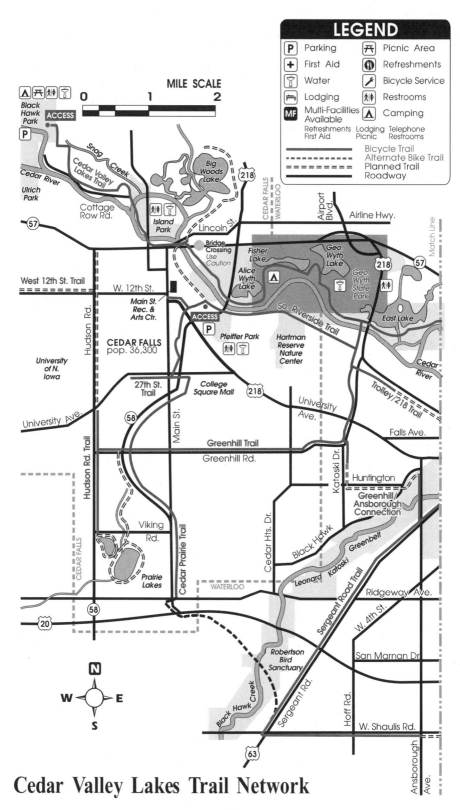

Cedar Valley Lakes Trail Network

Cedar Valley Lakes Trail Network

Trail Length	51.5 miles
Surface	Concrete, asphalt, limestone screenings, unimproved
Uses	Leisure bicycling, in-line skating, cross country skiing, hiking/jogging
Location & Setting	A recreations system uniting the park and recreation facilities of Waterloo and Cedar Falls. These two cities offer many cultural opportunities in addition to their excellent trails.
Information	Black Hawk County Conservation Board (319) 266-6813 2410 West Lone Tree Road Cedar Falls, IA 50613
	Eastern Iowa Tourism Association (800) 891-3482 P.O. Box 485 Vinton, IA 52349
County	Black Hawk

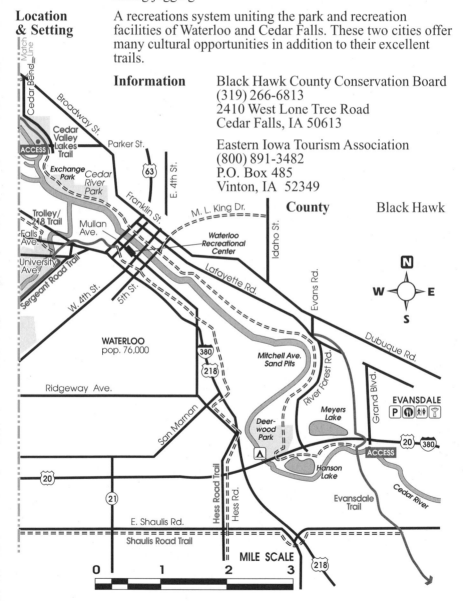

Cedar Valley Lakes Trail Network (Continued)

Recreation Trail	Miles	Width/Surface	Description/Accesses (•)	Water/Rest Rooms
CEDAR VALLEY LAKES TRAIL	2.70	10' ASPHALT	•BLACK HAWK PARK (ON WEST LONE TREE RD.) TO •ISLAND PARK (CENTER ST. NORTH OF CEDAR RIVER)	BLACK HAWK & ISLAND PARKS
	.60	10' CONCRETE	•ISLAND PARK TO THE CEDAR RIVER	ISLAND PARK
	3.80	8' ASPHALT/ 10' CONCRETE	CEDAR RIVER TO •GEORGE WYTH STATE PARK (ON 218 AT AIRPORT BLVD.)	STATE PARK
	.40	UNDEVELOPED GAP	PRIVATE LAND	
	1.65	10' ASPHALT & LIMESTONE	GREENHILL RD. TO •CEDAR BEND • HARTMAN RESV. (VIA SHIREY WAY)	
	5.25	10' HARD SURFACE	18TH ST. TO C.V.N.T. •DEERWOOD PARK, •CVNT TRAILHEAD	DEERWOOD PARK
CEDAR PRAIRIE TRAIL	5.10	10' CONCRETE	RIDGEWAY AVE. TO •GEORGE WYTH PARK, •PFIEFFER PK., •C.F. REC. CENTER, •CENTRAL PARK,•ROWND PARK	PFIEFFER & CENTRAL PARKS
	2.55	10' HARD SURFACE	RIDGEWAY AVE. TO US 63 (SERGEANT RD./SHAULIS TRAILS)	
GREENHILL TRAIL	4.80	10' CONCRETE	HUDSON RD. TO CEDAR RVR• VALLEY VIEW PARK & •HARTMAN RESERVES	PARKS
SOUTH RIVERSIDE TRAIL	2.30	10' ASPHALT	•PFEIFFER PK TO GREENHILL ROAD •HARTMAN RESV (VIA SHIREY WAY)	PFEIFFER PARK
TROLLEY/218 TRAIL	.50	10' LIMESTONE	GREENHILL RD. TO GRAND BLVD. (WEST OF HACKETT RD.)•CASTLE HILL PARK	
	.50	10' HARD SURFACE	GREENHILL RD TO •CASTLE BLUFF PK	
	1.56	10' HARD SURFACE	•CASTLE BLUFF PARK TO BLACK HAWK CREEK	
	.80	10' CONCRETE	BLACK HAWK CREEK TO •MULLAN AVE.	
	1.50	10' HARD SURFACE	MULLAN AVE. TO WEST 18TH ST. •DOWNTOWN PARKING LOTS	
SHAULIS ROAD TRAIL	2.25	15' ASPHALT/ 10' CONCRETE	•US. 63 (SERGEANT ROAD) TO ANSBOROUGH AVE.	
EVANSDALE TRAIL	1.60	10' LIMESTONE	RIVER ROAD •CVNT PARKING TO N. EVANS ROAD @ •CITY HALL	MEYER'S LAKE HARDEE'S
HUDSON RD. TRAIL	1.60	4' CONCRETE	UNIVERSITY AVE. TO VIKING ROAD	
27TH ST. TRAIL	.60	5' CONCRETE	COLLEGE ST. TO CEDAR PRAIRIE TRAIL	
	3.00	5' PAVED SHOULDER	UNION RD TO GRUNDY COUNTY LINE	
SERGEANT ROAD TRAIL	5.20	10' LIMESTONE	WESTFIELD AVENUE (218 TRAIL) TO SHAULIS ROAD •GREENBELT LAKE AT MARTIN ROAD	
GREENHILL/ ANSBOROUGH CONNECTION	2.60	10' HARD SURFACE	GREENHILL ROAD TO US 63 (SERGEANT ROAD TRAIL)	
WEST 12TH STREET TRAIL	1.50	10' HARD SURFACE	HUDSON ROAD TO UNION ROAD • BIRDSALL PARK	BIRDSALL PARK
HESS ROAD TRAIL	1.00	5' PAVED SHOULDER	SHAULIS ROAD TO ORANGE RD.	
MARTIN LUTHER KING TRAIL	1.20	10' CONCRETE	FRANKLIN STREET TO IDAHO STREET	

Waterloo Attractions

Rensselaer Russell House Museum — Mid-Victorian house for three generations of Russells. One of the oldest homes in Black Hawk County. **Location** 520 W. Third St.

Waterloo Museum of Art — Has a junior art gallery. **Location** 225 Commercial St.

Bluedorn Science Imaginarium — Experiment with physics, light, sound and momentum. Daily demonstrations, laser show, interactive exhibits. **Location** 322 Washington.

Grout Museum of History and Science — Daily planetarium shows, interactive "Discovery Zone". Learn about natural history & Native Americans. **Location** 503 South Street.

James & Meryl Hearst Center for the Arts — Two galleries featuring various exhibits throughout the year. **Location** 304 W. Seerley Blvd.

Victorian Home & Carriage House Museum — Built in 1861 and restored to elegant 1890 Victorian life. Gowned mannequins in period clothing. **Location** 300 W. 3rd.

Little Red Schoolhouse — 1909 one-room school with desks, blackboards, books, bell tower, pot-bellied stove, see a typical day in an old-fashioned school setting. **Location** First & Clay Streets.

Ice House Museum — Items used in harvesting, storing, and selling natural ice as in the early 1900's. A 1920s kitchen, horse drawn school hack, buggies, sleighs, a 1909 REO. **Location** First & Clay Streets.

Hartman Reserve Nature Center — 80 acre woodland in the heart of Black Hawk County. 5 miles of trails and three bridges, ideal for photography, hiking, x-c skiing & nature study. **Location** 657 Reserve Dr.

George Wyth House and Viking Pump Museum — Family home refurbished in the Art Deco style. Research library on the Art Deco period of 1925 to 1935 **Location** 303 Franklin St.

George Wyth State Park

Trail Length	3.8 miles
Surface	Asphalt, concrete
Uses	Leisure bicycling, in-line skating, cross country skiing, hiking/jogging
Location & Setting	One of the trails making up the Cedar Valley Lakes Trail Network. Located on the Cedar River within the Waterloo-Cedar Falls metropolitan area.
Information	George Wyth State Park (319) 232-5505

The park has a large expanse of woodland with many varieties of wildlife, with over 200 different species of birds observed and white-tailed deer year-round. Picnicking and camping facilities are available.

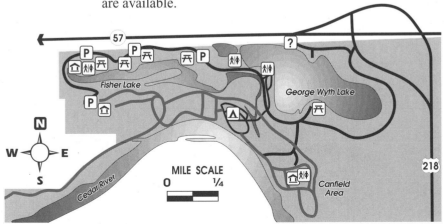

Cedar Valley Nature Trail

Trail Length	52.0 miles
Surface	Crushed limestone
Uses	Leisure bicycling, cross country skiing, hiking
Location & Setting	The trail is built on an abandoned rail bed between Cedar Rapids and Waterloo, Iowa. It's a nationally designated recreation trail and is part of the American Discovery Trail. Historical landmarks, archaeological sites and restored railroad depots at Gilbertville and Center Point add interest to the trail. Wildlife in the area includes deer, woodchucks, wild turkey, badgers and songbirds.
Information	Black Hawk County Conservation Board (319) 266-0328 2410 West Lone Tree Road Cedar Falls, IA 50613
	Linn County Conservation Board (319) 398-3505 1890 County Home Road Marion, IA
County	Black Hawk, Linn

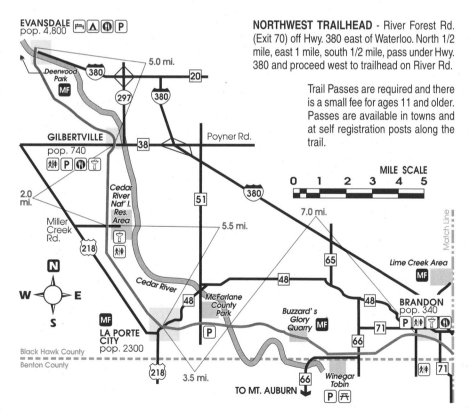

NORTHWEST TRAILHEAD - River Forest Rd. (Exit 70) off Hwy. 380 east of Waterloo. North 1/2 mile, east 1 mile, south 1/2 mile, pass under Hwy. 380 and proceed west to trailhead on River Rd.

Trail Passes are required and there is a small fee for ages 11 and older. Passes are available in towns and at self registration posts along the trail.

Recreation Parks

Wakema Park	Picnicking, water, restroom, parking, playground
Wild Cat Bluff Area	Boating, fishing, picnicking, camping, water, restroom, parking
Line Creek Area	Picnicking, camping, fishing, water, restrooms, shelter, parking
Winegar Tobin	Boating, fishing, picnicking, parking
McFarlane County Park	Picnicking, hiking, camping, fishing, shelter, water, restrooms, showers, parking, playground (138 acres).
Cedar River Natural Resource Area	Restroom, river access (540 acres)

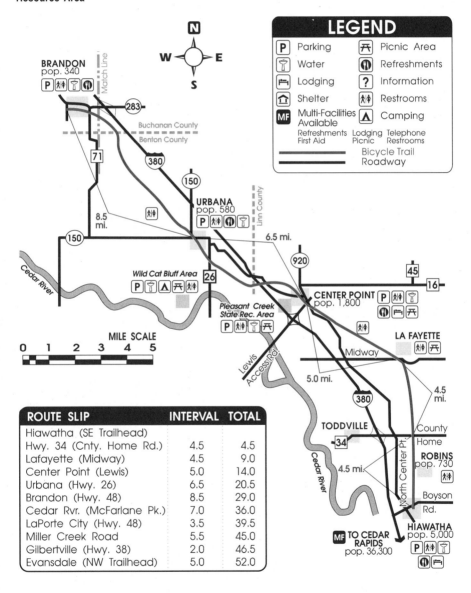

LEGEND

P	Parking	🍴	Picnic Area
🚰	Water	🍹	Refreshments
🛏	Lodging	?	Information
🏠	Shelter	🚻	Restrooms
MF	Multi-Facilities Available	🅰	Camping

Refreshments   Lodging   Telephone
First Aid   Picnic   Restrooms

────── Bicycle Trail
━━━━━━ Roadway

BRANDON pop. 340

URBANA pop. 580

Wild Cat Bluff Area

Pleasant Creek State Rec. Area

CENTER POINT pop. 1,800

LA FAYETTE

Midway

TODDVILLE

County Home

ROBINS pop. 730

Boyson Rd.

HIAWATHA pop. 5,000

MF **TO CEDAR RAPIDS** pop. 36,300

8.5 mi.

6.5 mi.

5.0 mi.

4.5 mi.

4.5 mi.

MILE SCALE
0 1 2 3 4 5

Cedar River

Buchanan County
Benton County

Match Line

Linn County

Lewis Access Rd.

North Center Pt.

ROUTE SLIP	INTERVAL	TOTAL
Hiawatha (SE Trailhead)		
Hwy. 34 (Cnty. Home Rd.)	4.5	4.5
Lafayette (Midway)	4.5	9.0
Center Point (Lewis)	5.0	14.0
Urbana (Hwy. 26)	6.5	20.5
Brandon (Hwy. 48)	8.5	29.0
Cedar Rvr. (McFarlane Pk.)	7.0	36.0
LaPorte City (Hwy. 48)	3.5	39.5
Miller Creek Road	5.5	45.0
Gilbertville (Hwy. 38)	2.0	46.5
Evansdale (NW Trailhead)	5.0	52.0

Cedar Valley Nature Trail

Davenport Area
Duck Creek Parkway Trail
Riverfront Trail

Trail Length	Duck Creek Parkway Trail .... 12.4 miles
	Riverfront Trail .... 5.0 miles
Surface	Asphalt and concrete
Uses	Leisure bicycling, in-line skating, cross country skiing, hiking/jogging
Location & Setting	Davenport/Bettendorf. Located in an urban greenbelt, combining woodlands, wetlands and urban housing surroundings. The terrain is flat and gently rolling.
Information	Davenport Parks & Recreation (319) 326-7812
	2816 Eastern Avenue
	Davenport, IA 52803
County	Scott

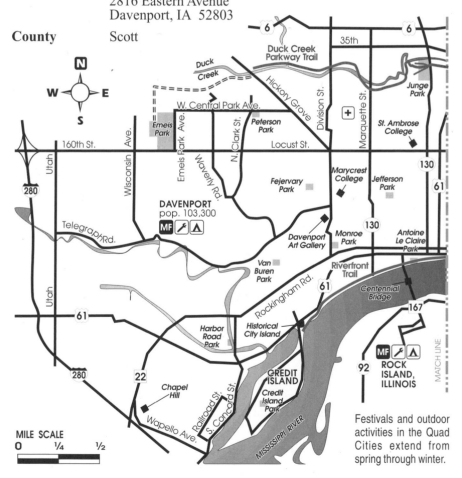

Festivals and outdoor activities in the Quad Cities extend from spring through winter.

The Duck Creek Parkway Trail follows the Duck Creek tributary from Emeis Park through Duck Creek Park to Central Avenue and Devil's Glen Park in Bettendorf.

The Riverfront Trail follows the Mississippi River from Mound Street to Credit Island Park.

LEGEND

▲	Camping	🐝	Picnic Area
✚	First Aid	🍴	Refreshments
🛏	Lodging	🔧	Bicycle Service
MF	Multi-Facilities Available	🚻	Restrooms

Refreshments Lodging Telephone
First Aid Picnic Restrooms

――――――― Bicycle Trail
========= Planned Trail
Roadway

Davenport Attractions

The Putnam Museum of History & Natural Science Mississippi River Valley wildlife, Asian & Egyptian galleries, 3500 year old mummy. **Location** 1717 W. 12th St.

International Fire Museum 1951 Mack pumper truck, hand drawn hose carts, uniforms, etc., all housed in a 1931 firehouse. **Location** 2301 E. 11th St.

Mississippi River Visitor Center Learn about the lock & dam system on the Mississippi and watch boats passing through Lock & Dam #15. **Location** Western tip of Arsenal Island.

Colonel Davenport Historic Home 1833 army fort construction that brought George Davenport here in 1816. **Location** Arsenal Island on the Mississippi River.

Davenport Museum of Art Closed Mondays & holidays. **Location** 1737 West 12th St.

Mississippi Valley Welcome Center On a scenic overlook, great view of the Mississippi River. Looks like an old riverboat captain's home. Brochures & information **Location**: 900 Eagle Ridge Rd., Le Claire.

Buffalo Bill Cody Homestead Home of the Cody family built in 1847. Restored home, stagecoach. **Location** 28050 230th Ave., Princeton.

Buffalo Bill Museum "Buffalo Bill" Memorial as well as a steamboat museum. **Location** 200 N. River Dr., Le Claire.

Davenport Area
Duck Creek Parkway Trail
Riverfront Trail

Decorah City Trails

Ice Cave Hill
Trail Length   1.25 miles

Surface/Setting   Ungroomed, moderate to difficult trails winding through pine and other native trees.

Uses   Fat tire bicycling, cross country skiing, hiking

Lower Ice Cave
Trail Length   1.0 mile

Surface/Setting   Natural, flat trail winding along the Upper Iowa River.

Uses   Fat tire bicycling, cross country skiing, hiking

Van Peenen Park
Trail Length   4.0 miles

Surface/Setting   Double-track, easy to moderate trails through native prairie and pine trees.

Uses   Fat tire bicycling, cross country skiing, hiking

Palisades Park
Trail Length   2.0 miles

Surface/Setting   Double-track, moderate to difficult. Trails show a spectacular view of Decorah. Picnic facilities are available.

Uses   Fat tire bicycling, cross country skiing, hiking

Oneota Drive Recreational Trail
Trail Length   2.5 mile

Surface/Setting   1.0 mile groomed double-track, easy to moderate. 1.5 mile asphalt - 8' wide. Trail winds along the Upper Iowa River and scenic Phelps Park bluffs.

Uses   Fat tire bicycling, cross country skiing, hiking

Twin Springs
Trail Length   .75 miles

Surface/Setting   Ungroomed trail overlooking Twin Springs trout stream. Moderate to difficult.

Uses   Fat tire bicycling, cross country skiing, hiking

Information   Decorah Parks and Recreation   (319) 382-4158
PO Box 513
Decorah, IA 52101

County   Winneshiek

Decorah Attractions

Vesterheim the Norwegian-American Museum America's oldest and largest museum devoted to one immigrant ethnic group. Vesterheim features objects from life in old Norway to the Atlantic Crossing to establishing life in pioneer America. Highlights are actual homes and buildings from Norway & pioneer immigrant America, the North Dakota prairie, a 25' ship sailed across the Atlantic, colorful costumes, hand-crafted decorative fold arts, fine arts by immigrant artists, a comprehensive display of pioneer immigrant farming equipment. **Location** 502 W. Water St.

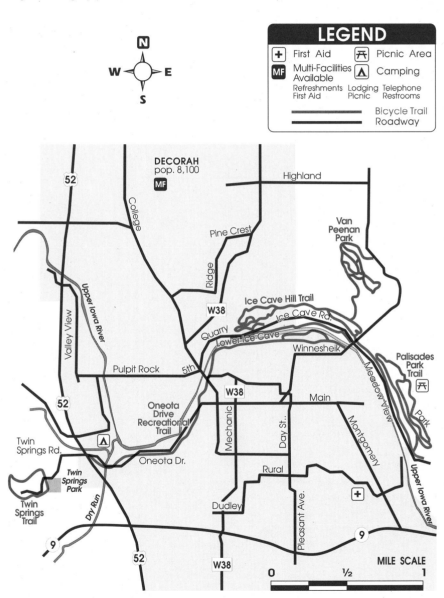

Decorah City Trails

Dubuque Area—Floodwall Trail

Trail Length	3.0 miles	*North section*	2.2 miles
		South section	.8 miles

Surface   Paved

Uses   Leisure bicycling, in line skating, cross country skiing, jogging

Location & Setting   Along the Mississippi riverfront in Dubuque. *North Section:* North to look at the dam. *South Section: Jones* Street east to parking by floodwall. Proceed south.

Information   Dubuque Visitors Bureau   (800) 798-8844
770 Town Clock Plaza—P.O. Box 705
Dubuque, IA 52004

County   Dubuque

AreaAttractions

Dubuque Iowa Welcome Center
Travel information along with rest facilities in Dubuque's historic Ice Harbor. **Location** Third St.

Cable Car Square — Cable Car elevator, charming shops, boutiques, and eateries. **Location:** 4th Street and Bluff St.

Fenelon Place Elevator Company The world's shortest, steepest scenic railway. From 4th St. to Fenelon Place. Magnificent view of three states and the Mississippi River. **Location** 512 Fenelon Pl.

Crystal Lake Cave — ¾ mile of well lit passageways with intricate formations and underground lake. The rare formations are known as anthrodites and the cave is a constant 50 degrees F.

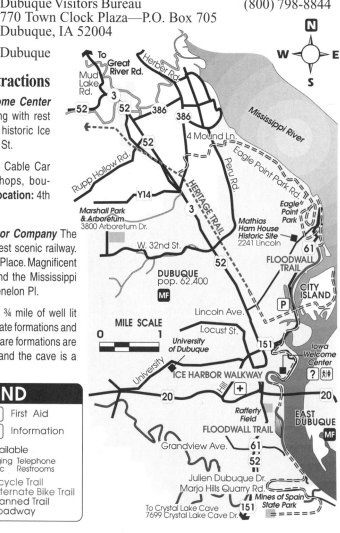

LEGEND

P	Parking	**+**	First Aid
♦♦	Restrooms	**?**	Information
MF	Multi-Facilities Available		

Refreshments   Lodging   Telephone
First Aid   Picnic   Restrooms

——————   Bicycle Trail
- - - - - - -   Alternate Bike Trail
= = = = = = =   Planned Trail
——————   Roadway

Great River Road Trail

Trail Length	16.0 miles
Surface	Concrete (road shoulder)
Uses	Tour biking, jogging
Location & Setting	Designated shoulders on either side of Hwy. X56 between Guttenberg and McGregor. Bluff lands, small communities.

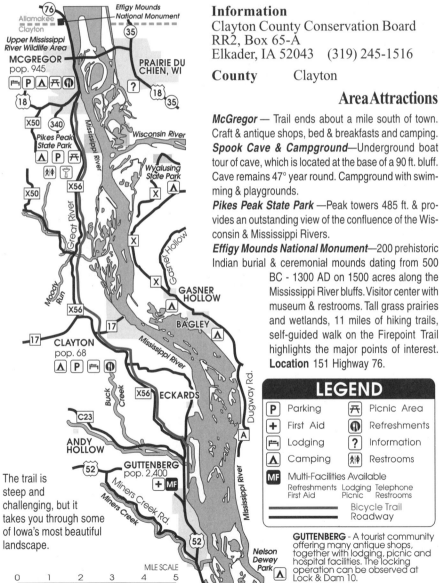

The trail is steep and challenging, but it takes you through some of Iowa's most beautiful landscape.

Information

Clayton County Conservation Board
RR2, Box 65-A
Elkader, IA 52043   (319) 245-1516

County   Clayton

Area Attractions

McGregor — Trail ends about a mile south of town. Craft & antique shops, bed & breakfasts and camping.

Spook Cave & Campground—Underground boat tour of cave, which is located at the base of a 90 ft. bluff. Cave remains 47° year round. Campground with swimming & playgrounds.

Pikes Peak State Park —Peak towers 485 ft. & provides an outstanding view of the confluence of the Wisconsin & Mississippi Rivers.

Effigy Mounds National Monument—200 prehistoric Indian burial & ceremonial mounds dating from 500 BC - 1300 AD on 1500 acres along the Mississippi River bluffs. Visitor center with museum & restrooms. Tall grass prairies and wetlands, 11 miles of hiking trails, self-guided walk on the Firepoint Trail highlights the major points of interest. **Location** 151 Highway 76.

LEGEND

P	Parking	**⛩**	Picnic Area
+	First Aid	**◍**	Refreshments
🛏	Lodging	**?**	Information
▲	Camping	**♟**	Restrooms
MF	Multi-Facilities Available		
	Refreshments Lodging Telephone First Aid Picnic Restrooms		
────	Bicycle Trail		
────	Roadway		

GUTTENBERG - A tourist community offering many antique shops, together with lodging, picnic and hospital facilities. The locking operation can be observed at Lock & Dam 10.

Heritage Trail

Trail Length	29.0 miles
Surface	Crushed limestone
Uses	Leisure biking, cross country skiing, hiking, snowmobiling
Location & Setting	Located in northeastern Iowa and built on a segment of the Old Chicago Great Western railbed. It runs westerly from just north of Dubuque to Dyersville. The trail provides rugged woodlands, river overlooks, limestone bluffs and primitive prairies. Trail Grade = 1% maximum.
Information	Swiss Valley Nature Center (319) 556-6745 13768 Swiss Valley Road Peosta, IA 52068
	Dubuque County Conservation Board (319) 556-6745
County	Dubuque

LEGEND

P   Parking   **🎋**   Picnic Area

🚰   Water   **🍴**   Refreshments

🛏   Lodging   **🚻**   Restrooms

MF   Multi-Facilities Available
Refreshments   Lodging   Telephone
First Aid   Picnic   Restrooms

――――――― Bicycle Trail
========= Planned Trail
Roadway

Along the trail are opportunities to visit interpretive sites, railroad artifacts, fossil collections, old lead mines and interesting communities.

Dyersville Attractions

The Ertl Company — Tour the plant of authentic toy replicas of tractors, planes, cars, trucks, etc. & toy store. **Location** Hwys. 136 & 20

Basilica of St. Francis Xavier — One of 33 basilicas in U.S. True medieval Gothic architecture. Designated a Basilica in 1956. Twin spires are 212 feet tall. **Location** Corner of 2nd St. SW & 1st Ave.

National Farm Toy Museum — Farm toys, trucks and other toys of interest. Displays illustrate the history and importance of agriculture. **Location** 1110 - 16th Ave. SE (Located at Hwy 136 & 20)

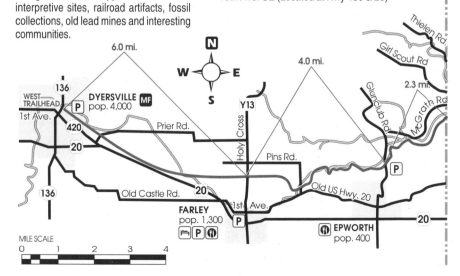

Dubuque Attractions

Mathias Ham House Historic Site—1833 Double log house with hands-on exhibit. 1856 Italian limestone mansion authentically restored and furnished. **Location:** 2241 Lincoln Ave.

Dubuque Museum of Art—National Historic Landmark offers a variety of exhibitions annually. The Wm. & Adelaide Glab Children's Gallery presents interactive, hands-on exhibitions. **Location:** 36 E. 8th St.

Dubuque Arboretum/Botanical Gardens—Award-winning garden displays flowers & vegetables, prairie grasses & wildflowers, water gardens, waterfalls & ornamental plantings. **Location:** 3800 Arboretum Dr.

Mississippi River Museum—Life-sized exhibits covering 300 years of river history. See the Sidewheeler William M. Black, a 277 ft. dredge boat now a National Landmark. **Location:** 3rd Street Ice Harbor.

For more information contact:
Tourist Information Center
(319) 556-4372
3rd St. & Ice Harbor
Dubuque, IA 52001

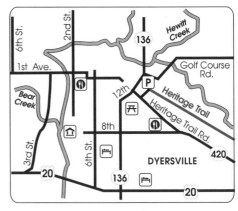

ROUTE SLIP	Interval	Total
Dubuque (1996 Completion)	0.0	0.0
East Trailhead	3.0	3.0
Durango	4.0	7.0
Graf	8.0	15.0
Epworth	4.0	19.0
Farley	4.0	23.0
Dyersville	6.0	29.0

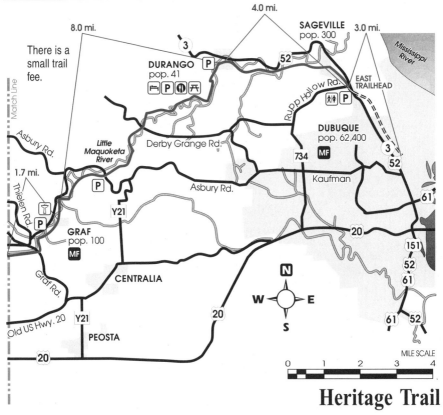

Heritage Trail

Hoover Nature Trail

Trail Length	39.5 miles (120 miles when complete)
Surface	Crushed limestone (where complete)
Uses	Bicycling, cross country skiing, hiking, horseback riding (restricted to marked paths)
Location & Setting	Located in southeast Iowa and built along abandoned railroad right-away. When completed it will span 6 counties and 16 towns from Cedar Rapids to Burlington.
Information	Hoover Nature Trail (319) 627-2626 Box 123 West Liberty, IA 52776
County	Blackhawk, Benton, Linn, Johnson, Muscatine, Louisa, Des Moines

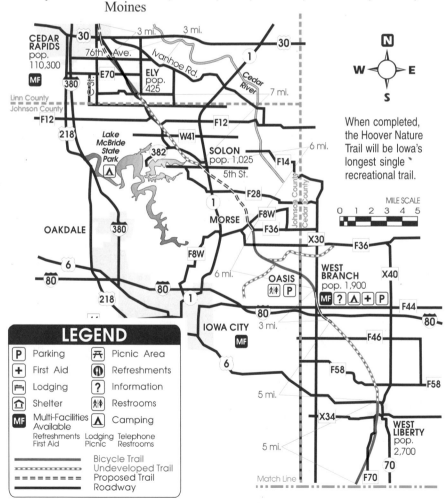

When completed, the Hoover Nature Trail will be Iowa's longest single recreational trail.

LEGEND

P	Parking	🎪	Picnic Area
+	First Aid	🍴	Refreshments
🛏	Lodging	?	Information
🏠	Shelter	🚻	Restrooms
MF	Multi-Facilities Available	A	Camping

Refreshments Lodging Telephone
First Aid Picnic Restrooms

Bicycle Trail
Undeveloped Trail
Proposed Trail
Roadway

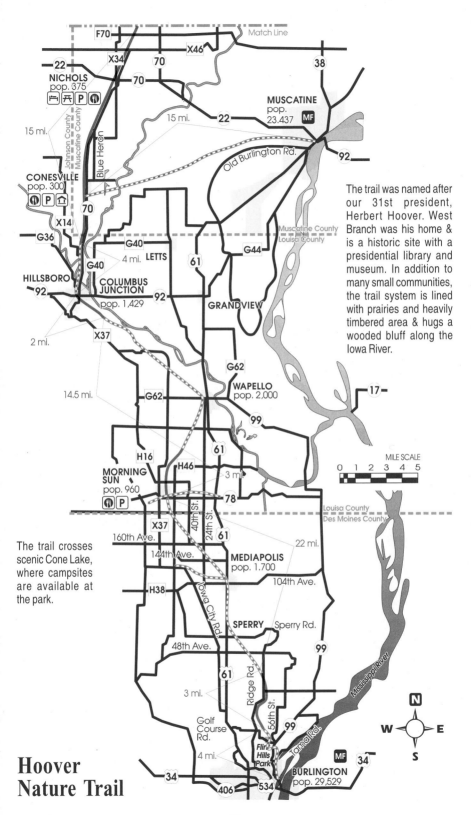

The trail was named after our 31st president, Herbert Hoover. West Branch was his home & is a historic site with a presidential library and museum. In addition to many small communities, the trail system is lined with prairies and heavily timbered area & hugs a wooded bluff along the Iowa River.

The trail crosses scenic Cone Lake, where campsites are available at the park.

Hoover
Nature Trail

Jackson County Trail

Trail Length	3.8 miles
Surface	Crushed limestone
Uses	Leisure bicycling, cross country skiing, hiking
Location & Setting	Built on abandoned railbed, the Jackson County Recreation Trail parallels the Maquoketa River with trailheads at Z34 and 45th streets just north of Spragueville. Spragueville is approximately 40 miles southeast of Dubuque via Hwy. 61 south and Hwy. 64 east.
Information	Jackson County Conservation Board (319) 652-3783 Courthouse Manquoketa, IA 52060
County	Jackson

Z20

Z20

Rockaway

Z34

Emergency Assistance
Jackson County Sheriff
(319) 652-3312

LEGEND

P Parking	🌐 Refreshments
▬▬▬ Bicycle Trail	
▬▬▬ Roadway	

VAN BUREN

Maquoketa River

Z20

45th St.

P

Main St.

SPRAGUEVILLE
pop. 150
🌐 Canoe Launch

Z34

MILE SCALE

0   1

113

64

PRESTON

N
W E
S

Views of scenic bluffs and overlooks along the trail provide striking views of the Iowa river valley. The area has numerous local parks, wildlife areas and preserve. Maquoketa Caves State Park has rugged hiking trails providing spectacular views of geological formations and caves to explore. Bellevue State Park's hiking trails include Indian burial mounds, a historic mill, a quarry and a butterfly garden. Spruce Creek Park features boating and camping.

Jefferson County Park

Trail Length	6.5 miles
Surface	Rock chips
Uses	Fat tire bicycling, cross country skiing, hiking
Location & Setting	Jefferson County Park is located just southwest of the town of Fairfield. The park entrance can be accessed off County Road H43 (south of Hwy. 34) or CR H33 (west of Hwy. 1).
Information	Jefferson County Conservation Board (515) 472-4421 2003 Libertyville Road Fairfield, IA 52556
County	Jefferson

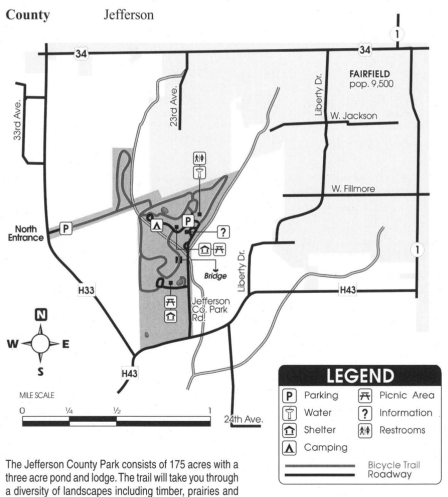

LEGEND

P	Parking	🌲	Picnic Area
🚰	Water	**?**	Information
🏠	Shelter	🚻	Restrooms
▲	Camping		
═══	Bicycle Trail		
───	Roadway		

The Jefferson County Park consists of 175 acres with a three acre pond and lodge. The trail will take you through a diversity of landscapes including timber, prairies and meadows. A 75 foot swinging bridge is featured on the trail connecting the picnic area with the camp area.

Kewash Nature Trail

Trail Length	13.8 miles
Surface	Crushed limestone
Uses	Leisure bicycling, cross country skiing, hiking
Location & Setting	Southeast Iowa, on a former railroad right-of-way running between the communities of Washington and Keota. The Kewash Nature Trail traverses a variety of landscape, from rich woodland area between Washington and West Chester to native prairie from West Chester to Keota.
Information	Washington County Conservation Board (319) 657-3457 2939 Hwy. 92 Ainsworth, IA 52201
County	Washington

There is a small trail fee for persons 16 years and older. Daily collection boxes are located at major road intersections.

LEGEND

P	Parking
A	Camping
Y	Water
🎋	Picnic Area
🔧	Bicycle Service
🚹🚺	Restrooms
MF	Multi-Facilities Available

Refreshments Lodging
Picnic Telephone
First Aid Restrooms

—— Bicycle Trail
—— Roadway

KEOTA pop. 1050

WEST CHESTER pop. 191

WASHINGTON pop. 7,100

Keoton
Pheasant Run
Badger Blvd.
Heyoka
Prairie Island
Far Horizons

W15
G26
W21
114
W21
92
G26
92
G36
1
W15
G38
W21
Dublin Dutch Creek
Far Horizons
Chester
Clemons Creek
Prairie Shadows
Dead Man's Curve
Crooked Creek
G38
92
1
Fox Hollow
Hays Timber
Valley
W38
GRACE HILL
TITU
Sunrise Lake

MILE SCALE
0   1   2   3   4

The trail provides the nature observer areas of rare and unusual plants such as silver sage, rattlesnake master, gentian, and blazing star. West of Washington, at Hays Timber, giant red oaks dominate the forest with their widespread branches.

Lake MacBride State Park

Trail Length	5 miles, plus several miles of trails limited to cross-country skiing and hiking.
Surface	Gravel
Uses	Bicycling, cross country skiing, hiking, snowmobiling
Location & Setting	East central Iowa just west of Solon and between Cedar Rapids and Iowa City.
Information	Lake MacBridge State Park
	3525 Hwy 382 N.E.
	Solon, IA 52333
County	Johnson

(319) 644-2200

During the spring and fall, shorebirds, waterfowl and ospreys are frequent visitors.

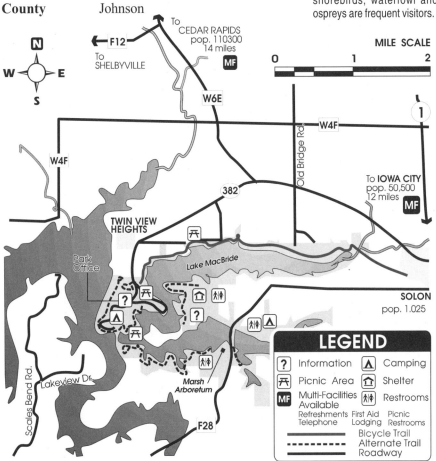

Lake MacBride State Park consists of 2,180 acres. In addition to an extensive trail system, facilities include both a modern and non-modern campground, beach area and concessions. Lake MacBride is a 812 acre artificial lake. Bird watchers will have the opportunity to sight nearly every songbird native to the region.

Pony Hollow Trail

Trail Length	4.0 miles
Surface	Crushed stone
Uses	Fat tire bicycling, cross country skiing, hiking, horseback riding, snowmobiling
Location & Setting	Town of Elkader in northeast Iowa. The trail forms a 'U' with the southwest trailhead commencing on the east side of Hwy. 13 and the north trailhead on the south side of Hwy 128.
Information	Clayton County Conservation Board (319) 245-1516 29862 Osborne Road Elkader, IA 52043-8247
County	Clayton

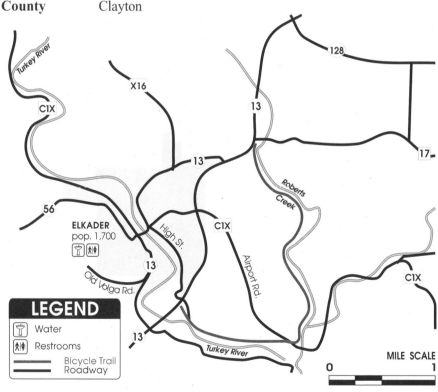

LEGEND

- Water
- Restrooms
- ——— Bicycle Trail
- ——— Roadway

MILE SCALE

0   1

Restroom, showers and electrical hook ups are available at the city park in Elkader. The Osborne Conservation Center is five miles south of Elkader on Hwy 13. It includes an Iowa Welcome Center, nature center, primitive campground, plus four hiking trails.

A state fish hatchery is located just north west of Elkader.

Prairie Farmer Trail

Trail Length	17.0 miles
Surface	Crushed limestone
Uses	Leisure biking, cross country skiing, hiking, snowmobiling (between Ridgeway & Cresco)
Location & Setting	The trail is built on the abandoned Milwaukee Railroad line between Calmer and Cresco The setting includes native prairie, wooded areas and farmland.
Information	Winneshiek County Conservation Board (319) 534-7145 2546 Lake Meyer Road Fort Atkinson, IA 52144
County	Winneshiek

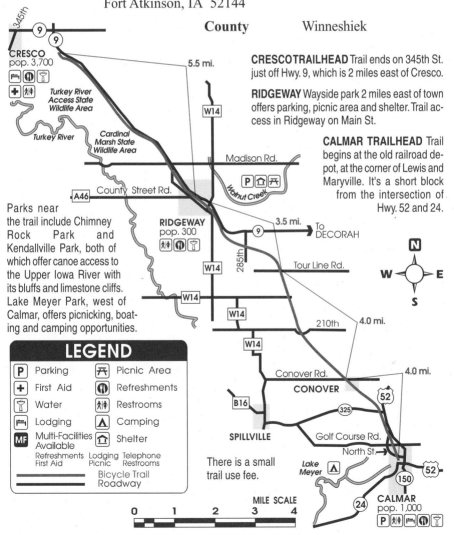

CRESCO TRAILHEAD Trail ends on 345th St. just off Hwy. 9, which is 2 miles east of Cresco.

RIDGEWAY Wayside park 2 miles east of town offers parking, picnic area and shelter. Trail access in Ridgeway on Main St.

CALMAR TRAILHEAD Trail begins at the old railroad depot, at the corner of Lewis and Maryville. It's a short block from the intersection of Hwy. 52 and 24.

Parks near the trail include Chimney Rock Park and Kendallville Park, both of which offer canoe access to the Upper Iowa River with its bluffs and limestone cliffs. Lake Meyer Park, west of Calmar, offers picnicking, boating and camping opportunities.

LEGEND

P	Parking	🎪	Picnic Area
+	First Aid	🍴	Refreshments
⛲	Water	🚻	Restrooms
🛏	Lodging	⛺	Camping
MF	Multi-Facilities Available	🏠	Shelter

Refreshments Lodging Telephone
First Aid Picnic Restrooms
━━━ Bicycle Trail
Roadway

There is a small trail use fee.

CRESCO pop. 3,700

Turkey River Access State Wildlife Area

Turkey River

Cardinal Marsh State Wildlife Area

Madison Rd.

County Street Rd.

Walnut Creek

RIDGEWAY pop. 300

To DECORAH

Tour Line Rd.

210th

Conover Rd.

CONOVER

SPILLVILLE

Golf Course Rd.

North St.

Lake Meyer

CALMAR pop. 1,000

MILE SCALE
0   1   2   3   4

5.5 mi.

3.5 mi.

4.0 mi.

4.0 mi.

Sac & Fox
Recreation Trail

Trail Length	7.5 miles
Surface	Packed dirt, mowed grass
Uses	Mountain biking, cross country skiing, hiking, horseback riding
Location & Setting	Located in south east Cedar Rapids from Cole Street to East Post Road. It runs through a deep forest valley for about half of the trail. The rest of the trail follows the Cedar River and is in more open terrain.
Information	Cedar Rapids Parks Department City Hall Cedar Rapids, IA 52401
County	Linn

(319) 398-5080

There is an admission charge to the Indian Creek Nature Center for non-members.

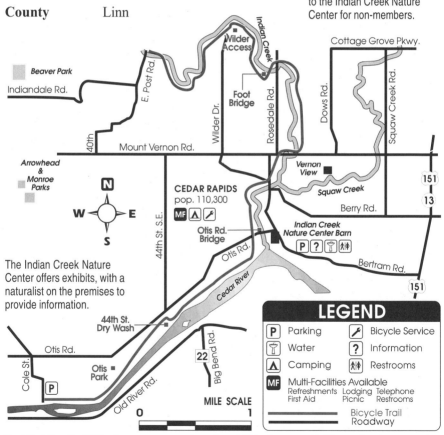

The Indian Creek Nature Center offers exhibits, with a naturalist on the premises to provide information.

LEGEND

P	Parking	🔧	Bicycle Service
💧	Water	?	Information
⛺	Camping	🚹🚺	Restrooms
MF	Multi-Facilities Available Refreshments Lodging Telephone First Aid Picnic Restrooms		

——— Bicycle Trail
Roadway

MILE SCALE
0   1

East Post Road to Wilder Access ·············· 1.5 miles   Wilder Access to Mt. Vernon Road ····· 2.0 miles
Mt. Vernon Road to Otis Road Bridge ········ 1.0 miles   Otis Rd. Bridge to 44th St. Dry Wash ·· 1.5 miles
44th St. Dry Wash to Cole St. parking lot ···· 1.5 miles   **Total   7.5 miles**

Shimek Forest Trail

Trail Length	4.5 miles (will be expanded to 6 miles)
Surface	Ballast, grass, dirt
Uses	Fat tire bicycling, cross country skiing, hiking
Location & Setting	Shimek State Forest consists of over 8,900 acres and is located east of Farmington in the southeast corner of Iowa. The trail is an abandoned railbed and can be accessed by exiting right on an old forest logging road, off road J58, northeast of Farmington.
Information	Shimek State Forest (319) 878-3811 Route 1, Box 95 Farmington, IA 52626
County	Van Buren, Lee

Check with the Forest Headquarters located north off J56 a short distance out of Farmington to determine alternate mountain biking opportunities in the Forest and nearby areas.

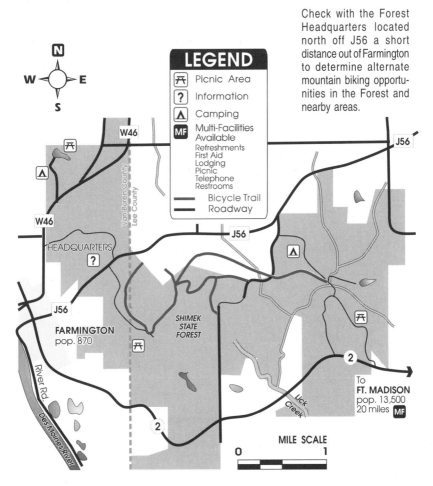

LEGEND

🏕 Picnic Area
❓ Information
🅰 Camping
MF Multi-Facilities Available
Refreshments
First Aid
Lodging
Picnic
Telephone
Restrooms
— Bicycle Trail
— Roadway

Sockum Ridge Park

Trail Length	10.0 miles (approx)
Surface	Grass, dirt
Uses	Fat tire bicycling, hiking
Location & Setting	Five miles southeast of Washington, one-half mile east off W55 at 305th Street.
Information	Washington County Conversation Board (319) 878-3811 2939 Hwy. 92 Ainsworth, IA 52201
County	Washington

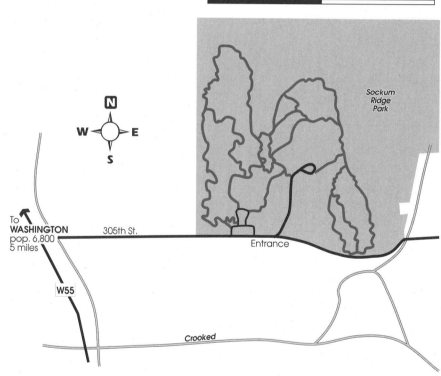

MILE SCALE

0   ¼   ½

N
W-E
S

Sockum
Ridge
Park

To WASHINGTON
pop. 6,800
5 miles

305th St.

Entrance

W55

Crooked

Sockum Ridge Park consists of 208 acres. The terrain is hilly, with forest and wetlands.

Park facilities include:
Parking, toilets and canoeing, but no water or camping.

Backbone State Park

Courtesy of Iowa Dept. of Natural Resources

Ken Formanek

A stone tower adjoins the boathouse and overlooks the lake.

Ken Formanek

A telling view of the "Devils Backbone" trail that give the park its name.

Mississippian-Age Amphibian Bone
was discovered within this unusually shaped limestone and shale-filled depression exposed in a quarry in southeastern Iowa.

The bone bed occurs in the middle of a unique sequence of rocks which were deposited in a depression formed within the flat-lying limestones and shales of the upper St. Louis Formation. The unusual dish-shaped configuration of the deposit led to closer inspection and to discovery of the fossils. The basal half of the deposit consists of angular-to-rounded blocks and boulders of St. Louis limestone in a shale matrix containing scattered bone. Overlying this is the bone bed, a semi-continuous to lenticular, bone-rich limestone conglomerate with thin interlayered shales, also rich in bone. Above the bone bed is a sequence of bedded limestones and minor shales containing fish remains, ostracodes and snails, but lacking fossils suggestive of normal marine conditions. At the edge of the depression, these limestones overlap and rest on top of the St. Louis and represent the top of the rock sequence in the quarry. Pleistocene glacial till overlies the rock in the quarry.

Courtesy of Iowa Dept. of Natural Resources

Bob McKay

Volga River State Recreation Area

Trail Length	30 miles
Surface	Natural
Uses	Fat tire bicycling, cross country skiing, hiking, horseback riding, snowmobiling.
Location & Setting	Two miles northeast of Fayette in northeast Iowa. The west entrance is one mile east of Hwy. 150 and the east entrance is 4 miles west of Wadena.
Information	Volga River State Recreation Area (319) 425-4161 10225 Ivy Road Fayette, IA 52142
County	Fayette

The park has 5,459 acres. The general area is often referred to as "Little Switzerland" because of its rugged topography, geologic features and substantial woods. The self-guided nature trail begins by the park office at the west entrance. Red fox, raccoon, skunk, opossum, muskrat, mine, beaver, white-tailed deer and wild turkey are all found in the area.

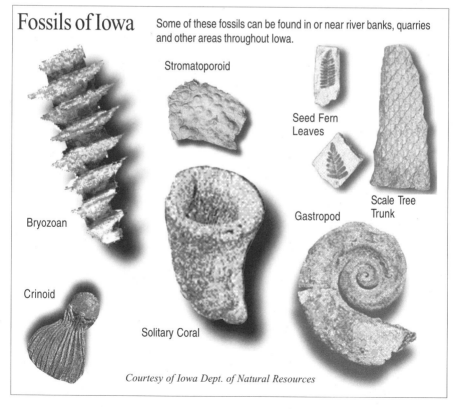

Fossils of Iowa

Some of these fossils can be found in or near river banks, quarries and other areas throughout Iowa.

Stromatoporoid

Seed Fern Leaves

Scale Tree Trunk

Gastropod

Bryozoan

Crinoid

Solitary Coral

Courtesy of Iowa Dept. of Natural Resources

Located 4 miles north of Fayette in scenic northern Iowa on the meandering Volga River. Site features campground with basic facilities and specified campsites. ELEVATION : 500 ft.

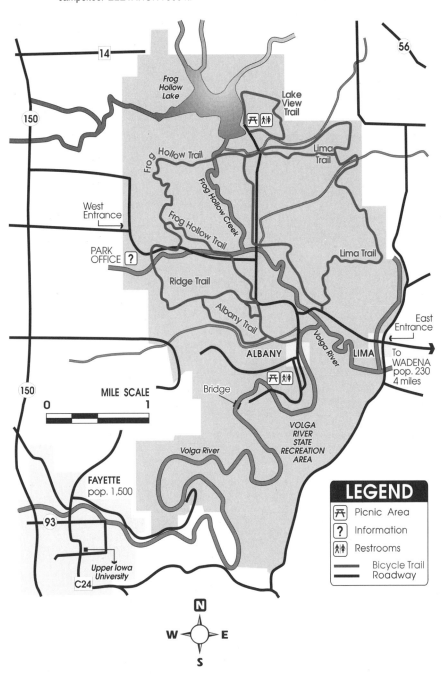

Volga River State Recreation Area

Yellow River State Forest

Trail Length	5 miles
Surface	Gravel, grass, dirt
Uses	Fat tire bicycling, cross country skiing, hiking
Location & Setting	Located in the northeast corner of the state, the biking trail is a segment of abandoned railbed. The forest can be accessed off Hwy. 76 about 10 miles southeast of Waukon or off Hwy. H, 2 miles west of Harpers Ferry.
Information	Yellow River State Forest (319)586-2548 RR I, Box 146A Harpers Ferry, IA 52146
County	Allamakee

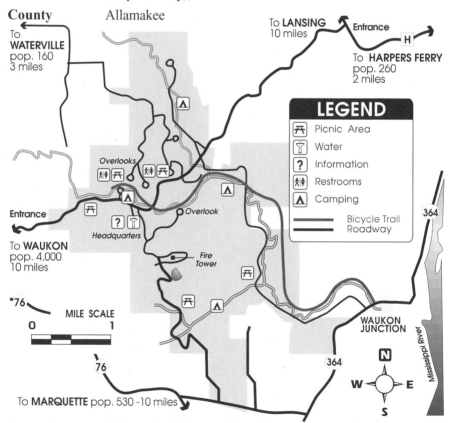

The forest covers some 6500 acres. In addition to the biking trail there are designated hiking and equestrian trails available. There are also fire lanes and logging roads that are not part of the trail system. There are trail logo signs, but, if you become disoriented, get to a road or fence and stay on it and it will eventually lead to help. Be sure to visit Effigy Mounds National Monument which borders the Mississippi River and is not far south on Hwy. 76.

Drinking water is available only at the sawmill and the headquarters area. There is a pay telephone with emergency numbers listed at a kiosk west of the headquarters.

Eastern Iowa
Additional Trails — Non-Illustrated

Discovery Trail

Trail Length	4.0 miles
Surface	Paved
Uses	Leisure bicycling, cross country skiing, in-line skating, jogging
Location & Setting	Clinton, Iowa. Trail is located along the Mississippi River, extending from Riverview Park on the south to Eagle Point Park on the North.
Information	Clinton Parks Dept. (319) 423-1260

Devil's Glen Park PLANNED

Trail Length	1.0 mile
Surface	Asphalt
Uses	Leisure bicycling, in-line skating, jogging.
Location & Setting	Bettendorf. Trail will run along Duck Creek through the park between Devil's Glen Drive to State Street.
Information	Bettendorf Parks Dept. (310) 359-1651

Indian Lake Park Trail

Trail Length	3.0 miles
Surface	Crushed rock
Uses	Leisure bicycling, cross country skiing, hiking, snowmobiling
Location & Setting	County of Van Buren, near the town of Farmington. Attractive trail area. Accessible from parking and camping areas within the park.

The Pikes Peak State Park overlook provides a spectacular view of the Mississippi River.

Photo courtesy of Iowa Dept. of Natural Resources

Mark Edwards

Kolonieweg Trail PLANNED 🚴🎿🚶

Trail Length	3 miles (*initial phase*)
Surface	Hard surface
Uses	Leisure bicycling, cross-country skiing, hiking
Location & Setting	Located in the Amana Colonies, nationally known as the home of one of America's most successful utopian communities, the trail connects the villages of Amana and Middle Amana. It will traverse along the Mill Race Canal, with parking, restroom and concessions available the Amana Depot trailhead.
Information	Amana Colonies Trails (319) 622-3639

Mad Creek Greenbelt 🚴🎿🚶

Trail Length	2.0 miles
Surface	Paved, crushed rock
Uses	Leisure bicycling, cross country skiing, jogging
Location & Setting	City of Muscatine in Muscatine County. Located by Lincoln Blvd. and along Hwy 38 on the north side. There is parking on both end of the trail. This is a Levy Trail. A Mississippi River overlook is part of the trail.
Information	Muscatine Parks Dept. (319) 263-0241

Old Creamery Trail PLANNED 🚴🎿🚶

Trail Length	15.3 miles
Surface	Limestone screenings
Uses	Leisure bicycling, cross-country skiing, hiking
Location & Setting	To be built on a former railroad corridor between Vinton and Dysar.
Information	Rails-to-Trails—Bob LaGrange (319) 472-4744

Pollmiller Park 🚴🚶

Trail Length	.7 miles Surface
Surface	Limestone
Uses	Leisure bicycling, jogging
Location & Setting	Lee County one half mile east of West Point. Trail connects West Point's South Park with Pollmiller Park.
Information	Lee County Conservation Board (319) 463-7673

Central Iowa Trails

Central Iowa Overview

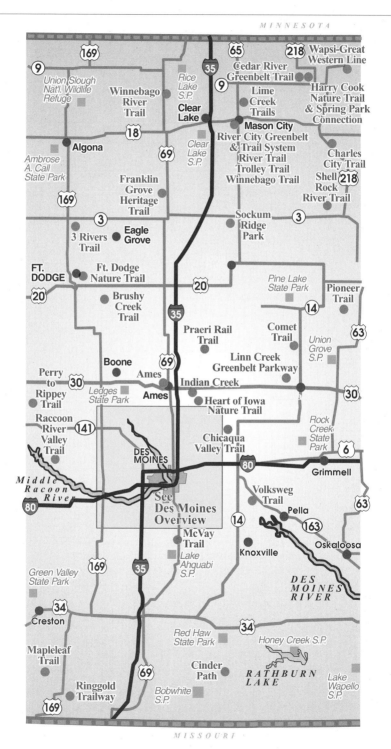

MINNESOTA

169
9
Union Slough Nat'l. Wildlife Refuge
Winnebago River Trail
Rice Lake S.P.
35
65
9
Cedar River Greenbelt Trail
218
Wapsi-Great Western Line
Lime Creek Trails
Harry Cook Nature Trail & Spring Park Connection
Clear Lake
Mason City
River City Greenbelt & Trail System
River Trail
Trolley Trail
Winnebago Trail
Charles City Trail
18
Algona
Clear Lake S.P.
69
Ambrose A. Call State Park
Franklin Grove Heritage Trail
Shell Rock River Trail
218
169
3
Eagle Grove
Sockum Ridge Park
3
3 Rivers Trail
FT. DODGE
Ft. Dodge Nature Trail
20
Pine Lake State Park
Pioneer Trail
20
Brushy Creek Trail
20
14
63
Praeri Rail Trail
Comet Trail
Union Grove S.P.
35
Boone
69
Linn Creek Greenbelt Parkway
Perry to
30
Ames
Indian Creek
Rippey Trail
Ledges State Park
Ames
Heart of Iowa Nature Trail
30
Raccoon River Valley Trail
141
Chicaqua Valley Trail
Rock Creek State Park
DES MOINES
80
6
Middle Racoon River
80
See Des Moines Overview
Volksweg Trail
Grimmell
14
Pella
63
McVay Trail
163
Oskaloosa
Green Valley State Park
169
Lake Ahquabi S.P.
Knoxville
DES MOINES RIVER
35
34
Creston
Red Haw State Park
34
Honey Creek S.P.
Mapleleaf Trail
69
Cinder Path
RATHBURN LAKE
Lake Wapello S.P.
Ringgold Trailway
Bobwhite S.P.
169

MISSOURI

Des Moines Overview

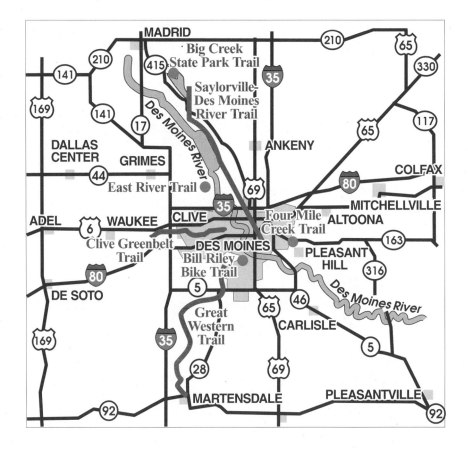

Des Moines Attractions

Des Moines Art Center Hours: Daily 11-5; Thur 11-9; Sun noon-5; closed Mon **Location** 4700 Grand Ave.

Adventureland Theme park with over 100 rides, shows, and attractions including 4 great roller coasters. Rides for all ages, from mild to wet and wild. Shows throughout the park feature a variety of family entertainment. **Location** Interstate 80 at Highway 65.

Basilica of St. John Designated a basilica in 1989. Northern Italian/Lombardy Romansque style, with gold leaf coffered ceilings, 46 stained glass windows, including 15 foot rose window. Ornate plaster and travertine marble interior. **Location** 1915 University Ave.

Des Moines Botanical Center On the east bank of the Des Moines River, one of the largest collections of tropical, sub-tropical and desert growing species in the U.S. **Location** 909 E. River Dr.

Hoyt Sherman Place Built in 1877 by pioneer businessman Hoyt Sherman, the home is a showcase for antiques and has a fine arts gallery and restored theater with domed ceiling. National Register of Historic Places. **Location** 1501 Woodland Ave.

Big Creek State Park

Trail Length	3.5 miles
Surface	Asphalt
Uses	Leisure bicycling, cross country skiing, in-line skating, hiking. *Horseback riding & snowmobiling are separate trails.*
Location & Setting	Eleven miles north of Des Moines and seven miles south of Madrid. Enter park area off Hwy. 415 on Beach Drive. Trail runs from Big Creek Beach south, connecting with the Saylorville-Des Moines River Trail for a total of 24 miles.
Information	Iowa Department of Natural Resources (515) 984-6473 Wallace State Office Building Des Moines, IA 50319-0034
County	Polk

LEGEND

🍴	Refreshments
?	Information
🚻	Restrooms
🏠	Shelter
——	Bicycle Trail
- - - -	Alternate
——	Roadway

To MADRID pop. 2,300 7 mi.

150th Ave.

146th Ave.

415

142nd Ave.

To ALLEMAN & I-35

Big Creek State Park

Big Creek State Park

138th Ave.

100th St.

415

72nd St.

126th Ave.

126th Ave.

Des Moines River

Park Stations

415

N **W** **E** **S**   MILE SCALE   0   1

Jester Pk. Rd.

Saylorville/Des Moines River Trail

To DES MOINES pop. 194,000 - 11 mi. & ANKENY 8 mi.

POLK CITY pop. 1,700

Big Creek State Park contains 3,550 acres with a 866 acre lake. Shelters and picnic area, a beach, two playgrounds and several boat ramps provide a variety of outdoor recreation opportunities. Refreshments are available at the beach during the swimming season.

Bill Riley Trail

Trail Length	1.2 miles, plus over 4 miles of connecting park roads.
Surface	Asphalt
Uses	Leisure bicycling, cross country skiing, in-line skating, hiking
Location & Setting	City of Des Moines. The north trailhead is located on 45th Street at the Ashworth Pool parking lot. The south trailhead is located at the Water Works Park, 2200 Valley Drive. The trail is flat and winds through Ashworth Park and along the Raccoon River providing great scenery.
Information	Des Moines Park & Recreation Dept. (515) 237-1386 3226 University Avenue Des Moines, IA 50311
County	Polk

The Bill Riley Bike Trail is a 1.2 mile trail in the heart of Des Moines. With connecting park roads, the length is over 5 miles. Nearby are the water works and Arboretum, Des Moines Art Center and the Science Center of Iowa. Bill Riley is an outdoor enthusiast and was a TV personality who organized the effort to build the trail in the 1970's. Future plans include connecting the Bill Riley to the Great Western Trail.

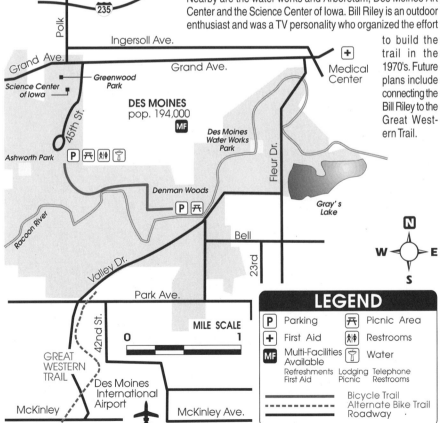

Brushy Creek Trail

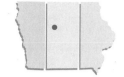

Trail Length	15.5 miles (multi-use) plus over 30 miles of planned trails
Surface	Natural - some of the trail groomed
Uses	Fat tire bicycling, cross-country skiing, hiking, equestrian, snowmobiling
Location & Setting	The Brushy Creek State Recreation Area is located five miles northeast of Lehigh on D46 and 15 miles southeast of Fort Dodge - Hwy 20 east to P73 and then south to entrance. It consists of 6500 acres of fields, woodland and stream valley.
Information	Brushy Creek State Recreation Area(515) 359-2501 R.R. 1, Box 150 Lehigh, IA 50557-7511
County	Webster

Nearby Attractions
Fort Dodge

Blanden Memorial Art Museum The first permanent municipal art gallery constructed in Iowa, located in Oak Hill Historic District. Regional, national and international exhibitions, distinctive collection of American, European and Asian art. Classes, workshops, films, lectures and special events such as the annual Oak Hill Art Festival. **Location** 920 Third Ave. South.

Fort Museum & Frontier Village 1862 military fort and frontier town, 10 original and replica buildings. Museum collection contains Native American, pioneer and military artifacts from the late 18th century to the present. Relive the area's history at Frontier Days in early June. **Location** Bus. 20 & Museum Rd.

Webster City

Kendall Young Library Doll Collection with 170 dolls dating from 1800-1890, Eberle statuettes, American Indian collection. **Location** 1201 Willson Ave.

Brushy Creek State Park

Photo courtesy of Iowa Dept. of Natural Resources

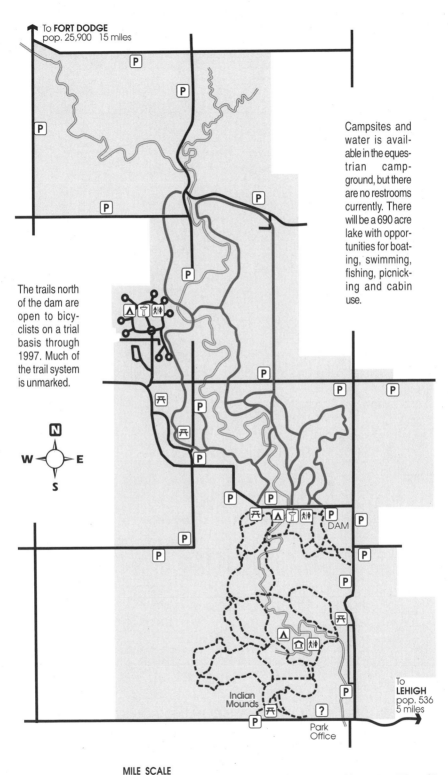

To **FORT DODGE**
pop. 25,900   15 miles

Campsites and water is available in the equestrian campground, but there are no restrooms currently. There will be a 690 acre lake with opportunities for boating, swimming, fishing, picnicking and cabin use.

The trails north of the dam are open to bicyclists on a trial basis through 1997. Much of the trail system is unmarked.

N
W E
S

DAM

Indian Mounds

To **LEHIGH**
pop. 536
5 miles

Park Office

MILE SCALE

0   ¼   ½   1

Brushy Creek Trail

Cedar River Greenbelt Trail Network

Cedar Valley
Harry Cook Nature Trail
Spring Park Connection

Trail Length	Cedar Valley .... 6.25 miles Harry Cook .... 2.00 miles Spring Park .... 0.75 miles
Surface	Crushed stone
Uses	Leisure bicycling, cross country skiing, hiking, horseback riding (Cedar River Greenbelt only)
Location & Setting	In Mitchell, at the southwest end of Cedar River Bridge near interstate Park. In Osage, there are accesses at Falk's Wildlife Area, off Highway 9, at Spring Park and at 1st Street south. The trails largely parallel the Cedar River. The setting is wooded and prairie with rolling scenery.
Information	Mitchell County Conservation Board (515) 732-5204 415 Lime Kiln Road Osage, IA 50461 Osage Parks and Recreation (515) 732-4674 114 South 7th Osage, IA 50461
County	Mitchell

Nearby Attractions Mason City

Kinney Pioneer Museum Fossils, dolls, ladies' fashions, soda shop. Conastoga wagon, Meredith Wilson collection, one-room school, log cabin, blacksmith shop, horse-drawn farm and fire fighting equipment. Antique cars. **Location** Municipal Airport entrance Hwy 18 W. Street.

Van Horn's Antique Truck Museum Large display of commercial vehicles from 1908 to 1931, large scale model circus, antique gas pumps, advertising signs. **Location** Hwy 65 North.

Lime Creek Nature Center 3501 Lime Creek Rd.

Frank Lloyd Wright Stockman House 1908 Prairie School house designed by Frank Lloyd Wright, the only middle-class house of his Prairie School period in the country open to the public. Furnished with Wright-designed furnishings. **Location** 530 First St. NE.

Charles H. MacNider Museum Tudor-style mansion overlooking Willow Creek features permanent collection of 19th & 20th century American art, the largest collection anywhere of puppets, marionettes and related props by the famous puppeteer Bill Baird. Exhibitions of sculptures, graphics, crafts, and paintings. **Location** 303 Second St. SE.

Grafton

Grafton Heritage Depot Turn of the century depot with waiting room, depot agents office, freight room. Upstairs houses local memorabilia. National Register of Historic Places. **Location** Main Street.

A variety of terrain, trees and plants can be observed along the trails. Wildlife consists of many varieties of animals and birds, including fox, hawks, owls, turkeys, egrets, beaver, mink and blue herons.

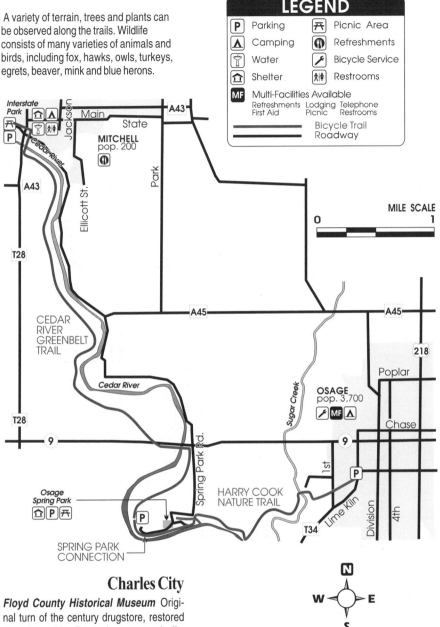

Charles City

Floyd County Historical Museum Original turn of the century drugstore, restored 1853 log cabin. For antique tractor buffs, collection of information pertaining to the founders of the gasoline tractor industry, the Hart-Parr Company. 1913 Hart-Parr tractor on display. **Location** 500 Gilbert Street.

Charles City Art Center 1904 Carnegie building houses art gallery, art library and classroom. Permanent collection plus other exhibits and programs. **Location** 301 N. Jackson Street.

Cedar River Greenbelt Trail Network
Cedar Valley
Harry Cook Nature Trail
Spring Park Connection

Chichaqua Valley Trail

Trail Length	20 miles
Surface	Crushed limestone
Uses	Leisure bicycling, cross country skiing, hiking, snowmobiling (Jasper County only).
Location & Setting	The trail crosses the forested banks and timbered bluffs of the Skunk River on an old railbed. The area offers a variety of scenic and diverse wildlife. Open spaces, farmland, wooded areas and small communities.
Information	Polk County Conservation Board (515) 999-2557 Jester Park Granger, IA 50109

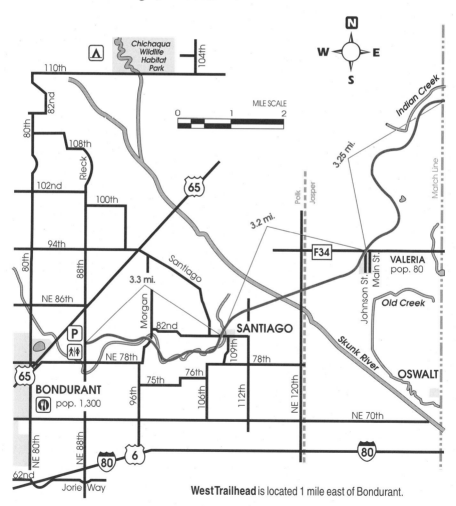

West Trailhead is located 1 mile east of Bondurant.

Information
(Continued)

Jasper County Conservation Board
115 N. Second Avenue, East
Newton, IA 50208

(515) 792-9780

County   Polk. Jasper

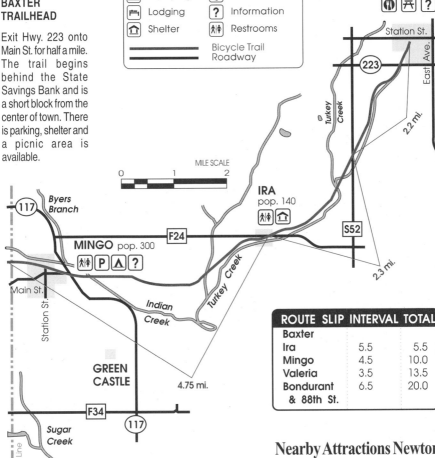

LEGEND

P Parking	🎋 Picnic Area
⚠ Camping	🍴 Refreshments
🛏 Lodging	? Information
🏠 Shelter	🚻 Restrooms
——— Bicycle Trail	
▬▬▬ Roadway	

BAXTER
pop. 951
see detail

BAXTER TRAILHEAD

Exit Hwy. 223 onto Main St. for half a mile. The trail begins behind the State Savings Bank and is a short block from the center of town. There is parking, shelter and a picnic area is available.

MILE SCALE
0   1   2

IRA
pop. 140

MINGO pop. 300

Byers Branch

Station St.

East Ave.

223

2.2 mi.

F24

S52

2.3 mi.

Turkey Creek

Indian Creek

Main St.

Station St.

GREEN CASTLE

4.75 mi.

F34

117

Sugar Creek

Match Line

ROUTE SLIP

	INTERVAL	TOTAL
Baxter		
Ira	5.5	5.5
Mingo	4.5	10.0
Valeria	3.5	13.5
Bondurant & 88th St.	6.5	20.0

N
W ⊕ E
S

TRAIL RULES

The trail is closed from 10:30 PM to 5:00 AM. Motorized vehicles and horses are not permitted on the trail. Snowmobiles are allowed on the Jasper County segment when snow cover is adequate.

Nearby Attractions Newton

Jasper County Historical Museum Washing machine display including the Maytag exhibit. 38 foot diorama depicting the history of Jasper County. 150 million year old dinosaur tracks. Victorian and 1930s era homes. Country store, church, school and blacksmith shop. Agricultural display in 1875 barn. Antique furniture store, post office. **Location** 1700 S. 15th Ave. W.

Chichaqua Valley Trail

Cinder Path

Trail Length	15.0 miles
Surface	Cinder
Uses	Leisure bicycling, cross country skiing, hiking
Location & Setting	South central Iowa between Chariton in Lucas County and Humeston in Wayne County. Built on abandoned railroad right of way. The trail is lined with native Iowa timber, with prairie areas and abundant wildlife.
Information	Lucas County Conservation Board (515) 774-2438 Box 78 Chariton, IA 50049
County	Lucas, Wayne

Adjoining the Cinder Path north of Chariton's Business 34 is the 1.5 mile Lucas County Conservation Exercise Trail, with 13 stations, from warm-up activities to aerobic activities and ending with cool-down muscle relaxers.

Access to the trail is available at any of the several intersecting county roads. An easy access is available at the east edge of Derby.

CHARITON
pop. 5,116

West Lake

Osceola Ave.

34

US 34

S23

Chariton River

To Red Haw Hill State Park

14

16th

3.5 mi.

3.5 mi.

Harts Mill Creek

Mormon Trl.

S23

To Red Haw Hill State Park

Chariton River

2.5 mi.

DERBY
pop. 171

P

65

US 65

306

Vine St.

2.5 mi.

Lucas / Wayne

H50

S23

H50

14

LEGEND

P	Parking		Picnic Area	
+	First Aid		Refreshments	
	Water		Bicycle Service	
	Lodging		Restrooms	
	Shelter		Camping	
MF	Multi-Facilities Available Refreshments Lodging Telephone First Aid Picnic Restrooms			

Bicycle Trail
Bikeway
------------ Alternate Bike Trail
========= Planned Trail
Roadway

N
W — **E**
S

65

US 65

1.5 mi.

HUMESTON

MILE SCALE
0   1   2   3

The even grade and smooth cinder surface of the Cinder Path makes the trail ideal for bikers and hikers. The path includes 16 wooden bridges, a covered bridge and a 20 foot lookout tower.

Clive Greenbelt Trail

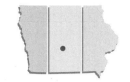

Trail Length	6.75 miles
Surface	Asphalt, crushed gravel
Uses	Leisure bicycling, cross country skiing, in line skating, hiking
Location & Setting	The Clive Greenbelt Trail is some 6.75 miles of scenic, heavily wooded trail through a greenbelt in the city of Clive, just west of Des Moines. The trail links with the Campbell Recreation Area which has concessions, picnic areas, restrooms and parking. There is a large selection of lodging and restaurants near the trail.
Information	Clive Park & Recreation Dept. (515) 223-6230
	9289 Swanson Boulevard
	Clive, IA 50325
County	Polk

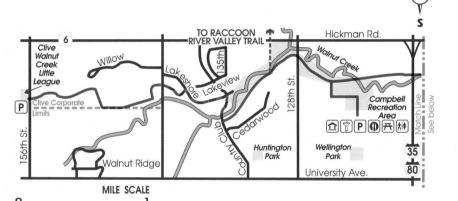

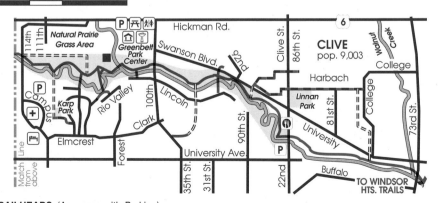

TRAILHEADS (Accesses with Parking)
1400 block of 86th St. (east trailhead) • 1500 block of 100th St. • 114th Street • NW 156th St. (west trailhead) • Campbell Recreation Area.

Comet Trail

Trail Length	6 miles
Surface	Crushed limestone (8' wide)
Uses	Leisure bicycling, cross country skiing, hiking
Location & Setting	From Conrad, through Beaman & east with a spur into Wolf Creek Recreation Area in Grundy County and a half mile into Tama County in Northeast Iowa. Built on a segment of the old Chicago and Northwestern line. Open areas, farmland, prairie, small communities.
Information	Grundy County Conservation Board (319) 345-2688 P.O. Box 36 Morrison, IA 50657
County	Grundy, Tama

Bicycle sales and service are available in Grundy Center, Hwy 14-175, 12 miles northwest of Beaman.

LEGEND

P	Parking	🎋	Picnic Area
+	First Aid	🍽	Refreshments
🚰	Water	🔧	Bicycle Service
🏠	Shelter	⛺	Camping
MF	Multi-Facilities Available		

Refreshments   Lodging   Telephone
First Aid   Picnic   Restrooms

▬▬▬▬▬ Bicycle Trail
▬▬▬▬▬ Undeveloped Trail
═══════ Planned Trail
▬▬▬▬▬ Roadway

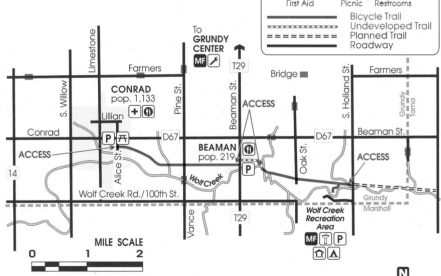

Accesses

Conrad	South end of Alice Street
Beaman	West side of County Road T-29. East side - 1/2 mile east of County Road T-29 and south.
Wolf Creek RA	Northeast corner of Wolf Creek Recreation Area (2 miles east and 1/2 mile south from Beaman)

East River Trail

Trail Length	5.5 miles
Surface	Asphalt
Uses	Leisure bicycling, cross country skiing, in-line skating, jogging
Location & Setting	Located in the city of Des Moines. The north trailhead is at McHenry Park (8th & Oak Park Ave.). The south trailhead is at Hawthorn Park (SE 14th & Railroad Ave.) Convenient accesses with parking at Birdland Park (Birdland Drive & Saylor Road) and at Crivaro Park (E. 1st and Grand Ave.).
Information	Des Moines Parks & Recreation (515) 237-1386 3226 University Avenue Des Moines, IA 50311
	Des Moines Visitors Bureau (515) 286-4950 601 Locust Des Moines, IA 50309
County Polk	

The trail follows the Des Moines River through the city, passing the Sec Taylor Baseball Stadium and the old Riverview Park. The north end of the trail connects to the Saylorville-Des Moines River Trail.

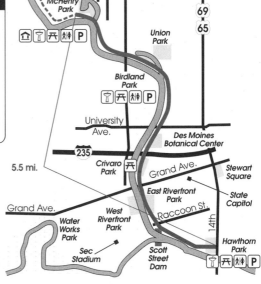

LEGEND

P	Parking	🎏	Picnic Area
🚰	Water	🔧	Bicycle Service
🏠	Shelter	🚻	Restrooms
MF	Multi-Facilities Available	⛺	Camping

Refreshments Lodging Telephone
First Aid Picnic Restrooms

——————— Bicycle Trail
- - - - - - - - Alternate Bike Trail
——————— Roadway

The East River Bike Trail's setting is primarily urban, but has ample park area and many features and points of interest, such as a 300' wooden boardwalk with an overlook of the river front, a botanical center and wildlife habitat.

MILE SCALE
0   1   2

Fort Dodge Nature

Trail Length	3.0 miles
Surface	Cinder
Uses	Leisure bicycling, cross-country skiing, jogging
Location & Setting	The nature trail is located between William's Drive and County Road D14 and built on abandoned railbed.
Information	Fort Dodge Parks Department (515) 576-7237 819 First Avenue, South Fort Dodge, IA 50501
County	Webster

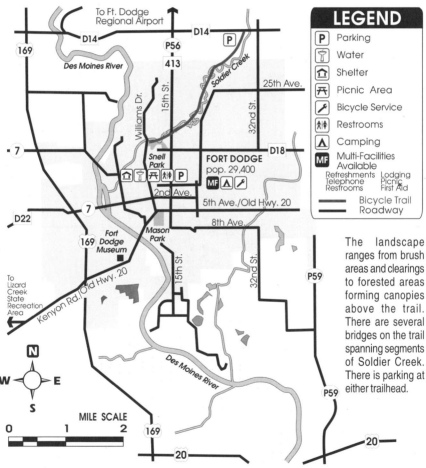

LEGEND

- **P**   Parking
- **T**   Water
- **⌂**   Shelter
- **⛱**   Picnic Area
- **🔧**   Bicycle Service
- **⚦**   Restrooms
- **⛺**   Camping
- **MF**   Multi-Facilities Available
  Refreshments   Lodging
  Telephone   Picnic
  Restrooms   First Aid
- ———   Bicycle Trail
- ———   Roadway

The landscape ranges from brush areas and clearings to forested areas forming canopies above the trail. There are several bridges on the trail spanning segments of Soldier Creek. There is parking at either trailhead.

One point of interest is the Fort Dodge Museum, which includes a pioneer village with collections of pioneer, military and Native American exhibits, and a replica of the Cardiff Giant, a famous hoax carved from a piece of Ford Dodge Gypsum.

Four Mile Creek Trail

Trail Length	3.8 miles (will be 35 miles when completed)
Surface	Paved, 12 feet wide
Uses	Leisure bicycling, cross country skiing, in-line skating, jogging
Location & Setting	The trail extends from the Four Mile Community Center at Easton Blvd. in Des Moines through Pleasant Hill to Scott Street in Pleasant Hill. It runs adjacent to Four Mile Creek.
Information	Polk County Conservation Board (515) 999-2557 Jester Park Granger, IA 50109
County	Polk

The trail will be 35 miles in length when complete & will connect the communities of Des Moines, Pleasant Hill, Altoona, Ankeny and Bondurant. It will be a vital link in the central Iowa "100 mile loop" which will connect many existing and proposed trails.

Enjoy the many attractions of Des Moines while in Iowa's Capitol City.

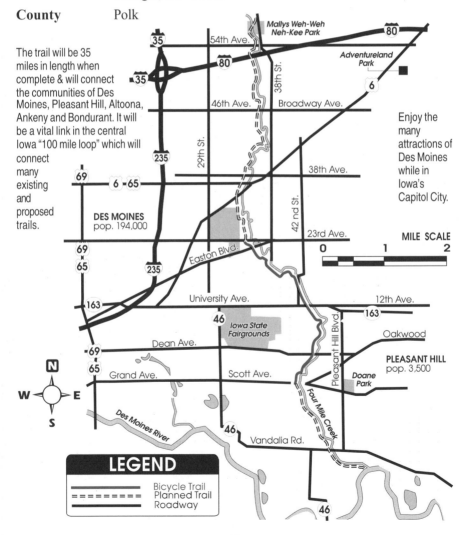

Franklin Grove Heritage Trail

Trail Length	1.8 miles
Surface	Asphalt
Uses	Leisure bicycling, in line skating, jogging
Location & Setting	Belmond, in north central Iowa. The trail is built on an abandoned railbed and runs north and south through the residential section of Belmond and into rural areas. There are accesses at street intersections.
Information	Belmond Chamber of Commerce (515) 444-3937 112 2nd Avenue NE Belmond, IA 50421
County	Wright

The city's facilities include bike repair, lodging and a park with a swimming pool, picnic tables, restrooms, water, shelter and concessions.

The trail through the residential area is landscaped with trees and shrubs with convenient benches. The north end of the trail is primarily native grasses while the south end is largely woodland and brush.

Great Western Trail

Trail Length	18.0 miles
Surface	Crushed limestone; asphalt near Martensdale.
Uses	Leisure bicycling, cross country skiing, hiking
Location & Setting	The trail was built on an abandoned segment of the Chicago Northwestern rail bed. The trail is relatively flat, with meadows, prairie grasses and an assortment of trees.

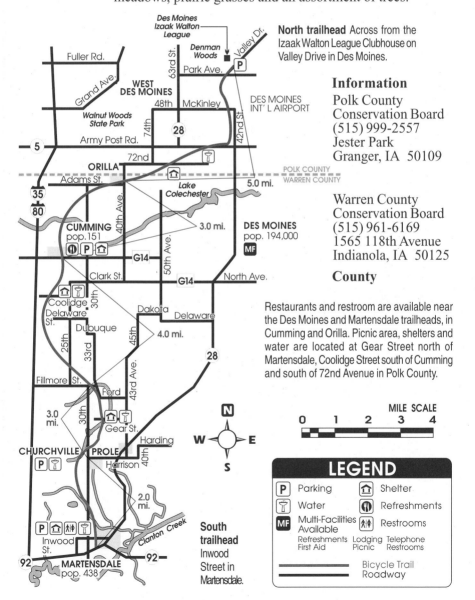

North trailhead Across from the Izaak Walton League Clubhouse on Valley Drive in Des Moines.

Information

Polk County
Conservation Board
(515) 999-2557
Jester Park
Granger, IA 50109

Warren County
Conservation Board
(515) 961-6169
1565 118th Avenue
Indianola, IA 50125

County

Restaurants and restroom are available near the Des Moines and Martensdale trailheads, in Cumming and Orilla. Picnic area, shelters and water are located at Gear Street north of Martensdale, Coolidge Street south of Cumming and south of 72nd Avenue in Polk County.

South trailhead Inwood Street in Martensdale.

MILE SCALE
0 1 2 3 4

LEGEND

P	Parking	🏠	Shelter
🍵	Water	🌐	Refreshments
MF	Multi-Facilities Available	🚻	Restrooms

Refreshments First Aid | Lodging Picnic | Telephone Restrooms

Bicycle Trail
Roadway

Heart of Iowa Nature Trail

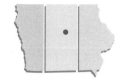

Trail Length	32 miles (11 completed)
Surface	Crushed limestone
Uses	Leisure bicycling, cross country skiing, hiking, snowmobiling and equestrian *(mowed turf adjacent to the limestone surface)*
Location & Setting	From Melbourne, west to Slater in Iowa's heartland. Built on an abandoned Milwaukee Railbed. There are significant prairie remnants east of Slater, heavily wooded tracts near Cambridge and Maxwell and wetland areas west of Cambridge.
Information	Story County Conservation Board McFarland Park, R.R. 2 Box 272V Ames, IA 50010 (515) 232-2516
	Marshall County Conservation Board 1302 E. Olive Street Marshalltown, IA 50158 (515) 754-6303
County	Story, Marshall

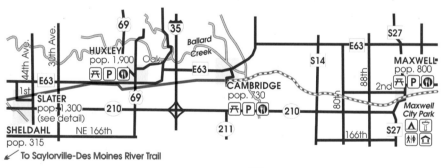

SLATER ACCESS
Trailhead is on R33 (Lynn St.) just north of town. There is parking. water. a picnic area and shelter available.

Future plans for the Heart of Iowa Nature Trail include connecting the west trail portion to the Saylorville-Des Moines Trail and the east trail portion to the Chichaqua Valley Trail, making a 100 mile loop.

LEGEND

- **P** Parking
- **A** Camping
- Water
- Shelter
- Picnic Area
- Refreshments
- Restrooms
- —— Bicycle Trail
- ••••••• Undeveloped Trail
- ===== Planned Trail
- —— Roadway

ROUTE SLIP	INTERVAL	TOTAL	POP.	ELEV.
Melbourne			1,312	1,040
Rhodes	4.8	4.8	367	1,011
Hoy Bridge	1.7	6.5		
Collins	5.1	11.6	45	1,005
Maxwell	5.0	16.6	783	885
Cambridge	7.0	23.6	732	871
Huxley	3.5	27.1	1,884	1,039
Slater	4.5	31.6	1,312	1,040

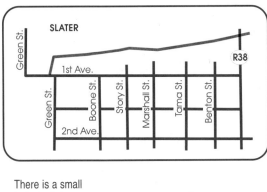

MELBOURNE ACCESS
Trailhead is at the corner of 290th and Hart but is undeveloped.

There is a small trail user's fee.

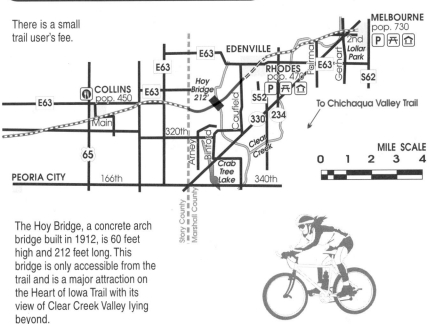

The Hoy Bridge, a concrete arch bridge built in 1912, is 60 feet high and 212 feet long. This bridge is only accessible from the trail and is a major attraction on the Heart of Iowa Trail with its view of Clear Creek Valley lying beyond.

Heart of Iowa Nature Trail

Lime Creek Trails

Trail Length	4.3 miles (loops)	
Surface	Natural, groomed	
Uses	Fat tire bicycling, cross-country skiing, hiking, horseback riding.	
Location & Setting	Two miles north of Mason City in north central Iowa. Access by bicycle by way of the Winnebago Trail out of Mason City or off Hwy. 65 by auto.	
Information	Cerro Gordo County Conservation Bd.	(515) 423-5309
	Lime Creek Nature Center 3501 Lime Creek Road Mason City, IA 50401	
County	Cerro Gordo	

Lime Creek Trails	Miles
Brewery Loop	.62
Badlands Loop	1.04
Old Stage Run	.97
Easy Access Trail	.57
River Bluffs Trails	1.07

The Lime Creek Nature Center consists of 400 acres of mixed species floodplain forest, old fields and a restored prairie.

The area is bounded on the east and north by the Winnebago River.

The education facility includes live and mounted animals, and various natural resource displays.. The park is closed to use from 10:30 p.m. to 6:00 a.m.

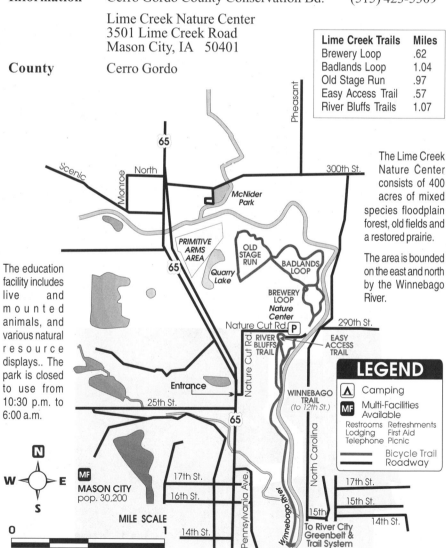

Linn Creek Greenbelt

Trail Length	8.0 miles	
Surface	Asphalt	
Uses	Leisure bicycling, cross country skiing, in-line skating. *Snowmobiling allowed adjacent to trail along bottom of dike.*	
Location & Setting	Marshalltown in central Iowa. It is built on the dike that runs along Linn Creek and the Iowa River, and links several Marshalltown parks and recreation areas.	
Information	Marshalltown Parks & Recreation Dept.(515) 754-5715 803 North 3rd Avenue Marshalltown, IA 50158	
County	Marshall	

The trail begins at the north trailhead in Riverview Park and currently ends at Morris Park, with plans for a 2 mile extension to the Marshall County Conservation Nature Center.

Parking is available at the trailheads and at the several parks lining the trail. There is a prairie area near the west end of the trail where prairie grasses and wild flowers can be observed.

Pioneer Trail

Trail Length	12.0 miles
Surface	Crushed limestone (grass surface for equestrian use)
Uses	Leisure bicycling, cross country skiing, hiking, equestrian
Location & Setting	Between Reinbeck and Holland in northeastern Iowa. Built largely on abandoned rail bed. Open areas, farmland, some wooded area, small communities.
Information	Grundy County Conservation Board (319) 345-2688 Box 36 Morrison, IA 50657
County	Grundy

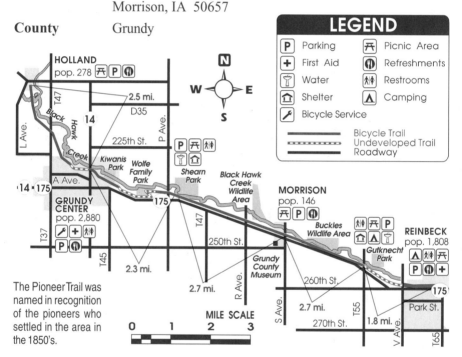

LEGEND

P	Parking	禾	Picnic Area
+	First Aid	①	Refreshments
▽	Water	徃	Restrooms
⌂	Shelter	▲	Camping
🔧	Bicycle Service		

——— Bicycle Trail
••••••• Undeveloped Trail
——— Roadway

HOLLAND pop. 278

GRUNDY CENTER pop. 2,880

MORRISON pop. 146

REINBECK pop. 1,808

Buckles Wildlife Area

Gutknecht Park

Black Hawk Creek Wildlife Area

Kiwanis Park

Wolfe Family Park

Shearn Park

Grundy County Museum

2.5 mi. — D35 — 225th St. — 2.3 mi. — 2.7 mi. — 2.7 mi. — 250th St. — 260th St. — 270th St. — 1.8 mi. — Park St. — 175

MILE SCALE
0   1   2   3

The Pioneer Trail was named in recognition of the pioneers who settled in the area in the 1850's.

Currently there is no public access between Grundy Center and just west of Reinbeck.

Grundy Center Attractions

Herbert Quick Schoolhouse One room county schoolhouse where noted Iowa author and publisher Herbert Quick attended school. Furnished with original items. **Location** Hwys 175 and 14.

Morrison Attractions

Grundy County Museum 1912 schoolhouse with historical, natural history and railroad displays, restored and furnished log cabin. **Location** 203 3rd St.

Black Hawk Creek Wildlife Area Swinging suspension bridge **Location** ¼ mile north of Morrison on County Road T-53.

Praeri Rail Trail

Trail Length	10.5 miles
Surface	Crushed limestone, mowed grass
Uses	Fat tire bicycling, cross-country skiing, hiking, horseback riding, snowmobiling.
Location & Setting	Built on abandoned railbed, this trail corridor runs from Roland through McCallsburg to Zearing in central Iowa. The trail parallels Hwy E18.
Information	Story County Conservation Board (515) 232-2516 McFarland Park R.R. 2 Box 272E Ames, IA 50010-9651
County	Story

Park hours are 5 a.m. to 10:30 p.m. Many segments of native prairie remnants can be seen adjacent to the trail.

The spelling of the work "Praeri" is in recognition of the area's strong Norwegian heritage.

Nearby Attractions Ames

Octagon Center for the Arts Changing exhibits and large museum gift shop. **Location** 427 Douglas.

Farm House Museum Built in the 1860's, the first building at IA State Agricultural College & Model Farm. Over 6,000 pieces of Victorian decorative arts & antique furnishings. **Location** 290 Scheman.

Reiman Gardens Wetland garden, entry courtyard, herb garden, rose garden and collections such as peonies, daylilies, iris. Annual garden flowers throughout the garden. The Education Center will offer workshops and meetings. **Location** Elwood Dr.; main entrance to campus from Hwy 30.

Brunnier Art Museum National and international art exhibitions, collections of glass, ceramics and art from Eastern and Western cultures, gallery talks, children's programs. **Location** 290 Scheman.

Panora Attractions

Turn of the Century Museum Features Guthrie County history with several buildings and exhibits, including, antique and artifact building, log cabin, general store, Milwaukee R.R. depot and caboose, church, one room country school, blacksmith shop, implement exhibit hall and coal mine display. Located in a park like setting on the SW side of Panora. **Location** 206 W. South St.

Area Events

May	Classic Bike Festival, promotes antique, classic & unique bikes.
June	*Redfield's* Old Settlers Day
July	*Yale* 4th of July Celebration
August	Panorama Days & *Adel's* Sweet Corn Festival
September	*Waukee* Fall Festival

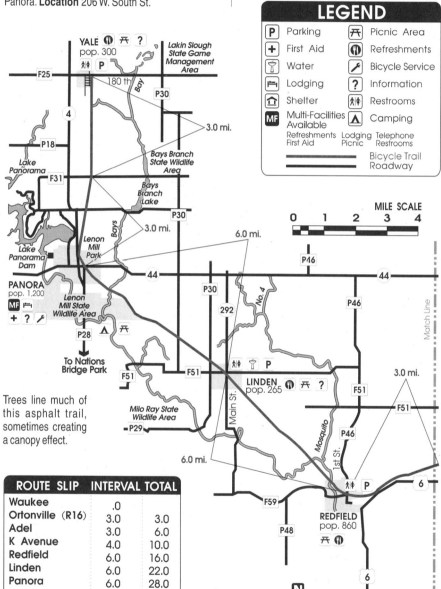

Trees line much of this asphalt trail, sometimes creating a canopy effect.

ROUTE SLIP	INTERVAL	TOTAL
Waukee	.0	
Ortonville (R16)	3.0	3.0
Adel	3.0	6.0
K Avenue	4.0	10.0
Redfield	6.0	16.0
Linden	6.0	22.0
Panora	6.0	28.0
Yale	6.0	34.0

Raccoon River Valley Trail

Raccoon River Valley Trail

Trail Length	34.0 miles
Surface	Asphalt
Uses	Leisure bicycling, cross country skiing, in-line skating, hiking
Location & Setting	Northwest of Des Moines between the towns of Waukee and Yale. The trail winds through the Raccoon River Greenbelt and is built on a former Chicago Northwestern rail bed.
Information	Dallas County Conservation Dept. (515) 465-3577 1477 K Avenue Perry, IA 50220
	Guthrie County Conservation Board (515) 755-3061 206 West South Street Panora, IA 50216
County	Dallas, Guthrie

You have the opportunity to tour six communities without leaving the trail, plus enjoy the prairie remnants, bottom land timber and wildlife habitat.

DALLAS CENTER

44

44

PANTHER

Match Line

Grade is 1% to 2%.

MILE SCALE

0   1   2   3   4

169

3.0 mi.

N.W. 46th Ave.

panther

P58

4.0 mi.

3.0 mi.

R16

3.0 mi.

R22

3.0 mi.

K Ave.

F51

? P

?

Adel Island Park

ORTONVILLE

6

6

ADEL **MF**
pop. 2,850

P58

WAUKEE
pop. 2,300

MF

R22

169

R16

80

N

W E

S

QUARRY

DE SOTO

VAN METER

BOONEVILLE

90

80

90

—71—

River City Greenbelt & Trail System
Trolley Trail
River City Trail
Winnebago Trail

Trail Length	**Total** .... **15.5 miles**
	River City Trail .... 8.5 miles
	Trolley Trail .... 5.0 miles
	Winnebago Trail ...... 2.0 miles
Surface	River City Trail .... paved, crushed limestone, city streets
	Trolley Trail .... asphalt
	Winnebago Trail ...... crushed limestone
Uses	Bicycling, cross-country skiing, in-line skating, hiking, jogging
Location & Setting	Mason City in north central Iowa. There are trailheads with parking at Milligan Park, at Elm and 13th Street and at Lime Creek Nature Center.

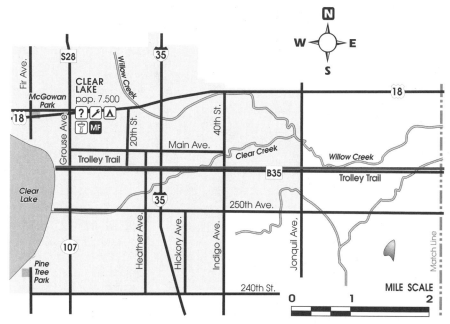

The Trolley Trail connects Mason City and Clear Lake. It runs parallel to County Road B35 and Mason City's electric trolley line which operates between the two cities. This is America's last working electric trolley.

Information   Mason City Parks & Recreation Dept.   (515) 421-3673
22 North Georgia
Mohawk Square
Mason City, IA 50401

County   Cerro Gordo

The River City Trail links Milligan and East Parks with cultural attractions of Mason City and its downtown areas. It follows along an abandoned railroad bed, parks and city streets. The downtown Riverwalk Trail is lighted. The Winnebago Trail proceeds north along the Winnebago River to the Lime Creek Nature Center. It offers picturesque views of the river's limestone bluffs as it transverses meadow and woods.

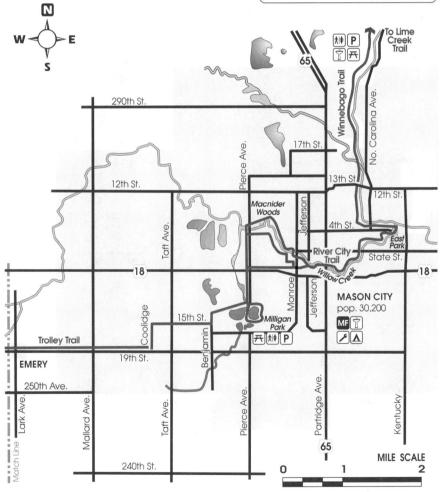

River City Greenbelt & Trail System

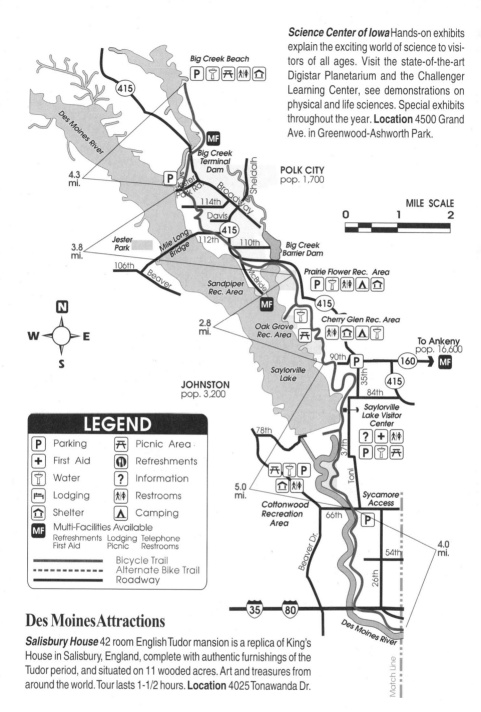

Science Center of Iowa Hands-on exhibits explain the exciting world of science to visitors of all ages. Visit the state-of-the-art Digistar Planetarium and the Challenger Learning Center, see demonstrations on physical and life sciences. Special exhibits throughout the year. **Location** 4500 Grand Ave. in Greenwood-Ashworth Park.

Big Creek Beach

415

Des Moines River

MF

Big Creek Terminal Dam

POLK CITY
pop. 1,700

4.3 mi.

P

Jester Park Rd.

114th

Broadway

Sheldalh

Davis

415

MILE SCALE

0   1   2

Jester Park

Mile Long Bridge

112th

110th

Big Creek Barrier Dam

3.8 mi.

106th

Beaver

McBride

Prairie Flower Rec. Area

P 🍽 🚻 🏕 🏠

Sandpiper Rec. Area

MF

415

Cherry Glen Rec. Area

N
W — **E**
S

2.8 mi.

Oak Grove Rec. Area

🍽 🚻 🏠 🏕 💧

90th

P

To Ankeny
pop. 16,600

160 → **MF**

35th

415

84th

Saylorville Lake

JOHNSTON
pop. 3,200

37th

Saylorville Lake Visitor Center

? **+** 🚻
P 💧 🍽

78th

🍽 💧 **P**
🏠 🚻

5.0 mi.

Cottonwood Recreation Area

66th

Toni

Sycamore Access

P

54th

4.0 mi.

26th

35 **80**

Beaver Dr.

Des Moines River

Match Line

LEGEND

P	Parking	🍽	Picnic Area
+	First Aid	🌀	Refreshments
💧	Water	**?**	Information
🛏	Lodging	🚻	Restrooms
🏠	Shelter	🏕	Camping

MF Multi-Facilities Available
Refreshments Lodging Telephone
First Aid Picnic Restrooms

——— Bicycle Trail
- - - - - Alternate Bike Trail
——— Roadway

Des Moines Attractions

Salisbury House 42 room English Tudor mansion is a replica of King's House in Salisbury, England, complete with authentic furnishings of the Tudor period, and situated on 11 wooded acres. Art and treasures from around the world. Tour lasts 1-1/2 hours. **Location** 4025 Tonawanda Dr.

Sherman Hill Historic District Elegant apartments, stately mansions and simple cottages from Victorian era and early 1900's in various stages of restoration. Group tours available. Self-guided tour brochure available at Wallace House. Annual fall house tour in September; winter tour first weekend in December. **Location** 756 16th St.

Saylorville-Des Moines River Trail

Saylorville-Des Moines River Trail

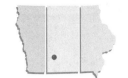

Trail Length	23.7 miles
Surface	Asphalt
Uses	Bicycling, cross country skiing, in-line skating, hiking
Location & Setting	The Saylorville-Des Moines River Trail follows the Des Moines River from the Birdland Marina in Des Moines, past Polk City to Big Creek Beach. The trail offers a variety of scenic vistas, including the Des Moines River Valley, Saylorville Lake, Big Creek Lake, prairies, ponds and forests. The upper segments provide rugged hills and valleys, while below Saylorville Dam, the grade is gently sloping.
Information	Des Moines Park and Recreation Dept. (515) 271-4700 3226 University Avenue Des Moines, IA 50311
County	Polk

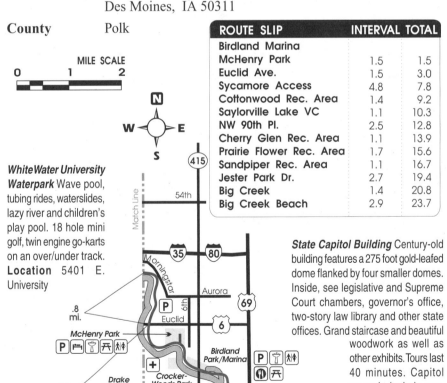

MILE SCALE

0   1   2

ROUTE SLIP	INTERVAL	TOTAL
Birdland Marina		
McHenry Park	1.5	1.5
Euclid Ave.	1.5	3.0
Sycamore Access	4.8	7.8
Cottonwood Rec. Area	1.4	9.2
Saylorville Lake VC	1.1	10.3
NW 90th Pl.	2.5	12.8
Cherry Glen Rec. Area	1.1	13.9
Prairie Flower Rec. Area	1.7	15.6
Sandpiper Rec. Area	1.1	16.7
Jester Park Dr.	2.7	19.4
Big Creek	1.4	20.8
Big Creek Beach	2.9	23.7

WhiteWater University Waterpark Wave pool, tubing rides, waterslides, lazy river and children's play pool. 18 hole mini golf, twin engine go-karts on an over/under track. **Location** 5401 E. University

Match Line

54th

.8 mi.

McHenry Park

3.0 mi.

Drake University

DES MOINES pop. 194,000

Drake Park

University Ave.

Crocker-Woods Park

Birdland Park/Marina

East River Bike Trail see page

State Capitol Building Century-old building features a 275 foot gold-leafed dome flanked by four smaller domes. Inside, see legislative and Supreme Court chambers, governor's office, two-story law library and other state offices. Grand staircase and beautiful woodwork as well as other exhibits. Tours last 40 minutes. Capitol grounds include gardens, sculptures, fountains and monuments. **Location** E. Ninth & Grand Ave.

Shell Rock River Trail

Trail Length	5.4 miles
Surface	Limestone screenings
Uses	Leisure bicycling, cross country skiing, hiking
Location & Setting	Between Clarksville and Shell Rock in north central Iowa. Access to the trail is located about 1/2 mile north of Hwy 3 near Shell Rock along Butler County Road T-63 . The northwest trailhead is located 2 miles southeast of Clarksville on a gravel road. There is parking.
Information	Butler County Conservation Board (319) 278-4237 28727 Timer Road Clarksville, IA 50619
County	Butler

Waverly Attractions

Iowa Star Clipper Dinner Train Three-hour dinner tour. Murder mysteries are offered monthly. **Location** 311 E. Bremer Ave.

The Waverly House/Bremer County Historical Society Museum Pioneer artifacts from Bremer County. **Location** 422 W. Bremer Ave.

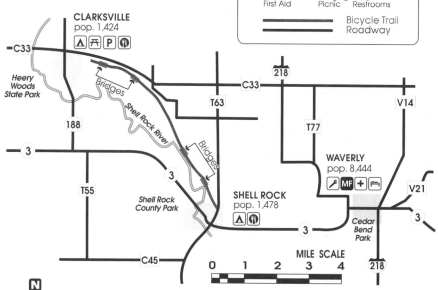

There is a city park located along the river in Shell Rock that can used as a beginning point. There are campgrounds with electrical and water facilities at the Shell Rock Recreation Area and Henry Woods State Park in Clarksville.

Glacial Boulders in Iowa

This 67 lb. nugget of native copper, tinged with greenish oxides, is one of the most distinctive glacial erratics found in Iowa and probably originated from the lake Superior area along the Upper Peninsula of Michigan. (Specimen is 15 inches long and 9 inches wide.) *Photo by Paul VanDorpe.*

This Black Hawk County field strewn with glacial erratics is typical of many pastures on the Iowan Surface of northeastern Iowa. *Photo by Pat Lohmann*

In western and southern Iowa, erratics generally lie buried beneath wind-deposited silts (loess) that cover the glacial materials. In these areas, erratics generally are restricted to valleys, where streams have eroded through the loess and into the underlying glacial deposits.

"Peculiar," "irregular," and "uncommon," are words used to describe one class of Iowa rocks—glacial boulders or "erratics." Geologists define erratics as stones or boulders that have been carried from their place of origin by a glacier and then left stranded by melting ice on bedrock of a different composition. In Iowa, glacial erratics are commonly observed where glacial deposits occur at the land surface, primarily in the north-central and northeastern parts of the state.

Glacial grooves and striations inscribe the limestone bedrock exposed in a Des Moines County quarry. These sets of parallel furrows and lines were gouged by glacial boulders embedded in the base of a slowly moving ice sheet. *Photo by Holmes Semken*

A large, weathered and rounded boulder of granite in this circa 1900 photograph of a Mason City neighborhood is a monument to the massive glacier that brought it south over 500,000 years ago. The nearest bedrock source of this erratic is central Minnesota. *Photo courtesy of The University of Iowa Calvin Collection.*

Excerpts by Raymond R. Anderson and Jean Cutler Prior Adapted from Iowa Geology 1990, No. 15, Iowa Department of Natural Resources

Three Rivers Trail

Trail Length	33.0 miles plus a spur running 6 miles south of Humboldt to Gotch State Park
Surface	Crushed limestone (10 feet wide)
Uses	Leisure bicycling, cross-country skiing, hiking, snowmobiling
Location & Setting	North central Iowa, built on abandoned railbed and running between the communities of Eagle Grove in Wright County through Humboldt County to Rolfe in Pocahontas County.
Information	Humboldt County Conservation Board (515) 332-4087 Courthouse Dakota City, IA 50529
County	Humboldt

Trail amenities include shelter houses, restrooms, access parking lots and picnic areas along the route.

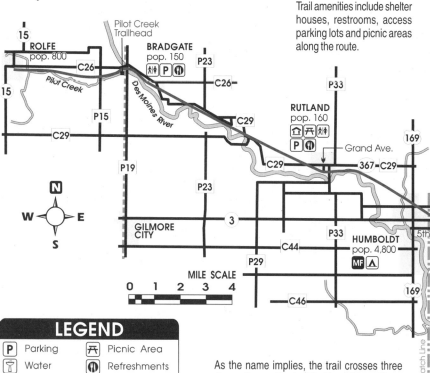

As the name implies, the trail crosses three rivers - the east fork of the Des Moines River, the west fork of the Des Moines River, and the Boone River. The western portion travels through beautiful timber with many scenic views of the west branch of the Des Moines River.

NEARBY PARKS WITH FACILITIES

Frank A. Gotch Park
4 miles south of Humboldt on Hwy 169. 1 mile east and 2 miles north. 67 acres with campsites, canoeing, fishing, boat ramp, showers, shelter, playground.

Humboldt Izaak Walton Park
1.5 miles west of Humboldt on Hwy 3. Features picnic areas, boat ramp, playground, fishing.

Lotts Creek Area
1/2 mile west of Livermore on 130th. A 30 acre park featuring campsites, picnic, wildlife area.

Oakdale Park
2.5 miles south and 1.5 miles east of Renwick. Features shelters, restroom, water, electric, picnic.

Joe Sheldon Park
1.75 miles west of Humboldt on Hwy 3. An 81 acre park featuring campsites, fishing, boat ramp, electric, showers, playgrounds, shelters.

Mileage increments	Miles
Eagle Grove to Humboldt County Line	3.0
County Line to P66	2.1
P66 to Long Tree Road	6.7
Lone Tree Road to 5 Street (Dakota City)	2.6
5 Street to Hwy 169 (Dakota City)	1.7
Hwy 169 to Grand Ave. (Rutland)	3.6
Grand Ave. to Saturn's (Bradgate)	7.4
Saturn's to Pilot Creek	0.7
Pilot Creek to Rolfe	5.2
Total	**33.0**
Spur from Humboldt to Gotch Park	*6.0*

The eastern portion of the trail passes through shrubby grasslands, marshy areas and open prairie. The trail has an abundance of remnant prairie sites with many species of wild flowers and grasses.

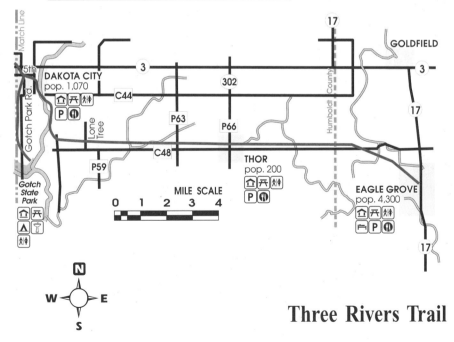

Three Rivers Trail

Volksweg Trail

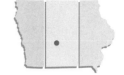

Trail Length	14.0 miles (10 miles completed)
Surface	Asphalt
Uses	Leisure bicycling, cross-country skiing, in-line skating, hiking/jogging
Location & Setting	Central Iowa, three mile south of Pella, which is and approximately 45 miles southeast of Des Moines on Hwy 163.
Information	Marion County Conservation Board (515) 828-2213 Courthouse - Fourth Floor Knoxville, IA 50138
County	Marion

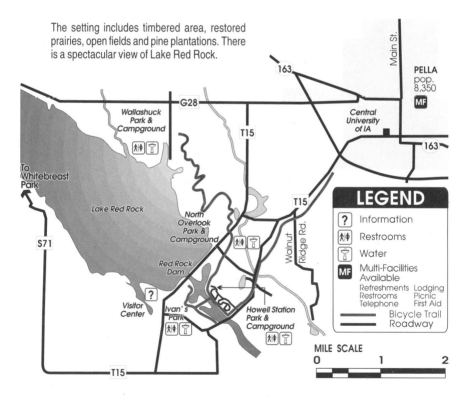

The setting includes timbered area, restored prairies, open fields and pine plantations. There is a spectacular view of Lake Red Rock.

LEGEND

? Information
Restrooms
Water
MF Multi-Facilities Available
Refreshments Lodging
Restrooms   Picnic
Telephone   First Aid
—— Bicycle Trail
—— Roadway

MILE SCALE
0   1   2

Volksweg is a Dutch work meaning "people's path". The Volksweg Trail is an asphalt paved trail with width varying from eight to ten feet. Most grades along the trail are less than 5%. However a few approach 7%. The section running from the North Tailwater Recreation Area to the Howell Station Recreation Area has a slope of less than 1%. The trail section connecting the city of Pella to the recreational areas of Lake Red Rock runs parallel to County Road T-15.

Wapsi-Great Western Line

Trail Length	4.0 miles (will be 10.5 miles when completed), plus 2 miles surrounding Lake Hendricks.
Surface	Crushed limestone (trail segment surrounding Lake Hendricks is mowed grass).
Uses	Leisure/Fat tire bicycling, cross-country skiing, hiking, snowmobiling
Location & Setting	Northeastern Iowa, extending north from Riceville. Straddles Howard and Mitchell Counties.
Information	Wapsi-Great West Line Committee (515) 985-4030 P.O. Box 116 Riceville, IA 50466-0116
County	Howard, Mitchell

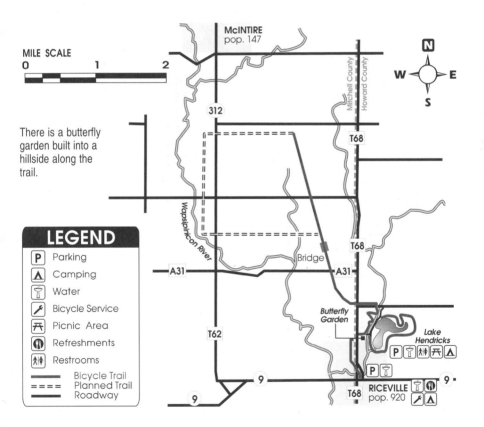

There is a butterfly garden built into a hillside along the trail.

LEGEND

- **P** Parking
- **A** Camping
- Water
- Bicycle Service
- Picnic Area
- Refreshments
- Restrooms
- —— Bicycle Trail
- ==== Planned Trail
- —— Roadway

The Wapsi-Great Western Line runs both on the Wapsipinicon River corridor and abandoned railbed. The trail traverses hilltops and rolling landscapes, native prairie and timber areas. The addition planned will add a large loop at the north end.

Central Iowa

Additional Trails — Non-Illustrated

Ames City Trails

Surface	Paved *unless otherwise noted*
Uses	Leisure bicycling, in-line skating, jogging

Location & Trail Length

Locations	Miles	
4th Street Path -S	1.1	Walnut to Beach Ave.
6th Street Path	0.6	Northwestern to Elwood Dr.
13th Street Path	1.0	Strange Rd. to Ridgewood Ave.
24th Street Path	1.1	Grand to Prairie View E., Prairie View to Edinburn Dr.
Beach Avenue Path	0.7	Lincoln Way to McCarthy Rd.
Brookside Park Path	0.6	Sixth& Grand to Harber; Harber to Pammel Dr.
ISU Paths	1.8	Pammel Dr. to Lincoln Way; Long to Strange; Wallace to Elwood Dr. Wallace to Knoll; Farmhouse Museum; Osborn Dr. to Farmhouse Museum; Osborn to Union Dr.; Memorial Union to Morril.
Lincoln Way Path	2.7	Thackley to Franklin; Franklin to Sheldon; Sheldon to Elwood
Pammel Drive Path	0.6	Hyland to Strange Rd.
Squaw Creek Path	1.5	S. 4th St. to ISU Research Park *(limestone)*
Strange Road Path	0.8	Blankenburg Dr. to Pammel Dr.

Information	Ames Chamber of Commerce 125 S. 3rd Ames, IA 50010	(515) 232-2310

Charles City Trail PLANNED

Trail Length	2.5 miles	
Surface	Asphalt - 8 feet wide	
Uses	Leisure bicycling, in-line skating, jogging	
Location & Setting	Charles City along the Cedar River, extending from Branting Ham Bridge to Hawkings Avenue with the city.	
Information	Charles City Parks Dept.	(515) 257-6312

Indian Creek Trail PLANNED 🚲🛼🚶

Trail Length	2.0 miles
Surface	Asphalt
Uses	Leisure bicycling, in-line skating, jogging
Location & Setting	City of Nevada. The trail will follow Indian Creek for the entire length of the city.
Information	Nevada Parks Dept. (515) 382-4352

Maple Leaf Pathway 🚲⛷️🚶🧲🏂

Trail Length	2.5 miles
Surface	Crushed rock
Uses	Leisure bicycling, cross-country skiing, hiking, horseback riding, snowmobiling
Location & Setting	Ringgold County with a trailhead starting in Diagonal. It is built on a former railroad right-of-way.
Information	Ringgold County Conservation Board (515) 464-2787

McVay Trail 🚲🛼🚶

Trail Length	1.6 miles
Surface	Asphalt
Uses	Leisure bicycling, in-line skating, jogging
Location & Setting	City of Indianola in Warren County. The trail goes through a residential area with trailheads at Pickard Park and behind Hardees on 5th Street.
Information	Indianola Parks and Recreation Dept. (515) 961-9420

Perry to Rippey Trail

Trail Length	9.0 miles
Surface	Ballast, grass, dirt
Uses	Fat tire bicycling, cross-country skiing, hiking, snowmobiling
Location & Setting	Between Perry and Rippey through three counties: Greene, Dallas and Boone. Trail is located on an abandoned railroad right-of-way and is adjacent to highway a major portion of its length.
Information	Greene County Conservation Board (515) 386-4629 Dallas County Conservation Board (515) 465-3577 Boone County Conservation Board (515) 353-4237

Ringgold Trailway

Trail Length	3.0 miles
Surface	Crushed rock, natural-groomed
Uses	Fat tire bicycling, cross-country skiing, hiking, horseback riding, snowmobiling.
Location & Setting	East of Mount Ayr in Ringgold County. Built on a former railroad right-of-way. A trailhead is located in Poe Hollow Park, a popular multi-recreational area.
Information	Ringgold County Conservation Board (515) 464-2787

Winnebago River Trail

Trail Length	3.5 miles (plus a 1 mile hiking trail and 1.8 miles unimproved)
Surface	Crushed stone, ballast (paving with asphalt planned)
Uses	Leisure bicycling, cross-country skiing, hiking
Location & Setting	Forest City in Winnebago County. There is an interpretive trail open to fat tire bicycling around the marsh area in Thorpe Park, 5.5 miles west of Forest City.
Information	Winnebago County Conservation Board (515) 565-3390

Explanation of Symbols

ROUTES

━━━━━ Biking Trail
▬▬▬▬ Bikeway
▬ ▬ ▬ ▬ Alternate Bike Trail
▪▪▪▪▪ Undeveloped Trail
■ ■ ■ ■ Alternate Use Trail
═ ═ ═ ═ Planned Trail
━━━━━ Roadway

TRAIL USES

 Mountain Biking

 Leisure Biking

 In Line Skating

 (X-C) Cross-Country Skiing

Hiking

Horseback Riding

Snowmobiling

FACILITIES

🔧 Bike Repair

🏕 Camping

➕ First Aid

❓ Info

🛏 Lodging

🅿 Parking

⛱ Picnic

🍹 Refreshments

🚻 Restrooms

⌂ Shelter

⛲ Water

MF Multi Facilities Available

Refreshments   First Aid
Telephone   Picnic
Restrooms   Lodging

ROAD RELATED SYMBOLS

(45) Interstate Highway

(45) U.S. Highway

45 State Highway

45 County Highway

AREA DESCRIPTIONS

Parks, Schools, Preserves, etc.

Waterway

Mileage Scale

Directional

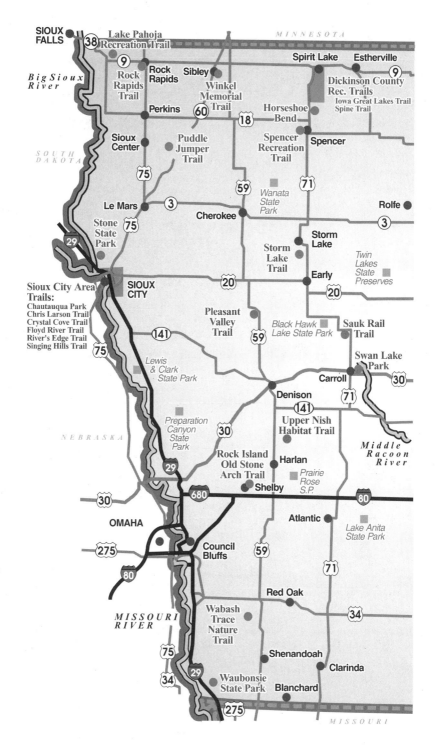

Western Iowa Overview

Jerry Leonard

Stone State Park is one state park hosting a state preserve within its boundaries.

Photo courtesy of Iowa Dept. of Natural Resources

Dickinson County Recreation Trails
Spine Trail
Iowa Great Lakes Area Bike Routes

Trail Length	10.5 miles (7.5 miles completed)
Surface	Asphalt
Uses	Leisure bicycling, cross-country skiing, in-line skating, hiking
Location & Setting	Northwest Iowa. The south trailhead is in Milford and extends from 23rd and Keokuk Street to Spirit Lake, primarily on abandoned rail corridor.
Information	Dickinson County Conservation Board (712) 338-4786 1013 Okoboji Avenue Milford, IA 51351
County	Dickinson

In addition to the trail, this map includes some sixty miles of signed routes on low traffic country roads. The Terril Loop is 31 miles long and designated by signs with a red dot. There are trailheads at the DNR boat ramp in Arnold and at the southern end of the Spine Trail in Milford. The Superior/Swan Lake Loop is 29 miles long and designated by signs with a blue dot. It has trailheads in Superior or at Minnewaukon State Park on the Iowa/Minnesota border.

LEGEND

P	Parking	🎪	Picnic Area
🛏	Lodging	🍴	Refreshments
⛺	Camping	🔧	Bicycle Service

▬▬▬▬ Bicycle Trail Bikeway
= = = = = Planned Trail
Roadway

WETLANDS — Fen, Dickinson County

Fens are Iowa's most unique wetland type. They are found primarily along the margins of the freshly glaciated landscapes in north-central Iowa and scattered throughout northeastern Iowa. These wetlands are sustained by groundwater flow and include saturated peat deposits, often in mounded positions along hill slopes and stream terraces. The water is highly mineralized compared to most wetlands, and, as a result, fens contain numerous state-listed rare and endangered species. Because of their unique hydrology, fens are unlikely

candidates for restoration projects, and the few that still remain need to be protected. With each passing year, more people are realizing the value associated with the preservation of natural wetland systems. These sites are recognized not only for their recreational and wildlife benefits, but increasingly for their importance as part of the natural hydrologic cycle. The management and restoration of Iowa's wetlands needs to be a co-operative venture among all segments of the state's scientific community.

Photo by Carol Thompson

Courtesy of Iowa Department of Natural Resources

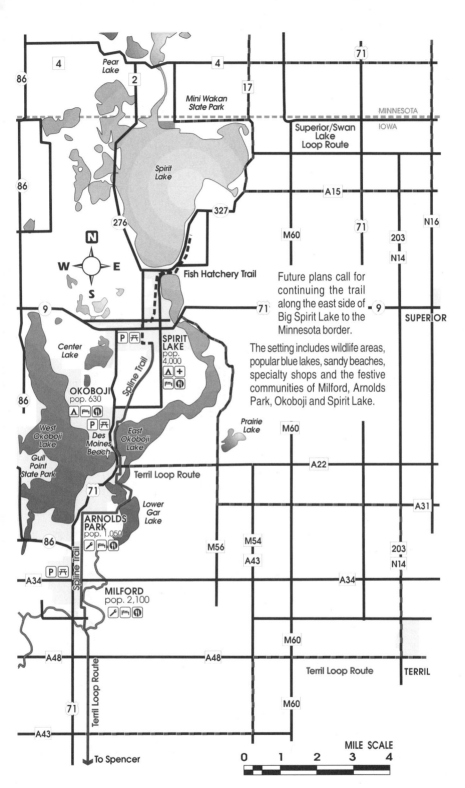

Future plans call for continuing the trail along the east side of Big Spirit Lake to the Minnesota border.

The setting includes wildlife areas, popular blue lakes, sandy beaches, specialty shops and the festive communities of Milford, Arnolds Park, Okoboji and Spirit Lake.

Dickinson County Recreation Trails

Lake Pahoja Recreation Trail

Trail Length	3.7 miles *Bicycling is currently limited to 1.4 miles on the north side of the lake.*
Surface	Asphalt for 1.4 miles, the remainder is grass
Uses	Leisure bicycling, cross-country skiing, in-line skating, jogging/hiking
Location & Setting	Northwest corner of Iowa, 20 miles from Sioux Falls, South Dakota and 5 miles south of Larchwood. Exit Hwy. 182 to Hwy. A26 to access road.
Information	Lyon County Conservation Board (712) 472-2217 311 First Avenue, East Rock Rapids, IA 51246
County	Lyon

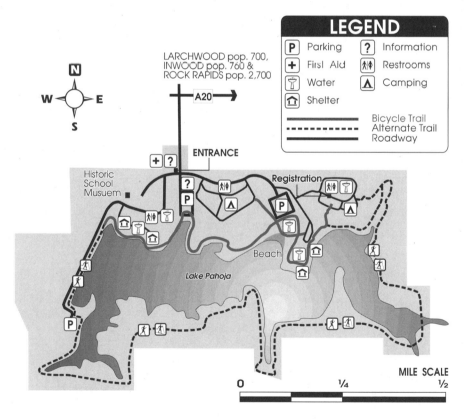

Lake Pahoja Recreation Area is a 232 acre highly developed, multi-use recreation area. Facilities include two lodges, playgrounds, campgrounds, beach and boat ramp. The lake is 72 acres.

Pleasant Valley Trail

Trail Length	2.5 miles (over 5 miles when complete)
Surface	Concrete
Uses	Leisure bicycling, in-line skating, jogging
Location & Setting	Ida Grove. The trail is constructed on flood control right-of-way and runs from the high school and then follows Badger Creek, and along Maple River and Odebolt Creek, then back to the high school, forming a loop.
Information	City of Ida Grove (712) 364-2428 P.O. Box 236, Ida Grove, IA 51445
County	Ida

The trail utilizes the berm along three rivers, which provide beauty and wildlife. It could potentially be joined to the Sauk Rail Trail in Sac County. Ida Grove is located in western Iowa, about 40 miles east of Sioux City.

Rock Island Old Stone Arch

Trail Length	3.3 miles
Surface	Asphalt - 10 feet wide
Uses	Leisure bicycling, in-line skating, jogging.
Location & Setting	The trail begins in Shelby on the south at Hwy I-80, exit #34 and follows the former Chicago, Rock Island & Pacific line to a 6 acre timber area in southwest rural Shelby County. The city of Shelby is 20 miles northeast of Council Bluffs.
Information	City of Shelby (711) 544-2404 419 East Street Shelby, IA 51570
County	Shelby

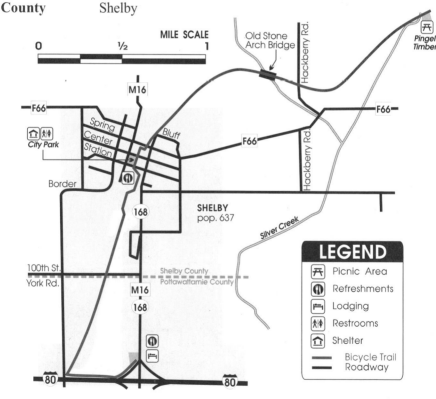

The trail crosses a 1869 30 foot high limestone trestle, adjacent to the city's recreational facilities, and two pony truss bridges. There are several wooded areas along the route.

Salt and Pepper Sands of Western Iowa

The modern Missouri River drains a vast area of the American West, with many of its tributaries having headwaters in the Rocky Mountains. The Missouri forms Iowa's western border with Nebraska, and its channel has repeatedly shifted course across the broad north-south valley, which exceeds 15 miles wide in places. Unravelling the geologic evolution of this major valley to its present location has become an important element in the assessment of groundwater resources in western Iowa.

This tooth from a Stegomastodon, a distinctly Pliocene-age member of the ancient elephants, came from gravels at Akron, in Plymouth County, and places the age of this western-derived alluvium at 1.6 to 4.0 million years old (length is 9 inches). *Photo by Tim Kemmis*

Reconstructing the ancestry of the Missouri drainage system involves various lines of geologic evidence. To establish a relative time framework, geologists must investigate the relationships between the various glacial-age deposits that lie above bedrock as well as the evidence of erosional gaps separating them. In general, these deposits consist of a complex sequence of glacial drift left by advances of continental ice sheets from the north at least eight times between about 500,000 and 2.5 million years ago. In addition, rivers deposited large amounts of sand and gravel during melting of these various glaciers as well as during warmer interglacial episodes like today. These buried deposits of sand and gravel are of particular importance to parts of western Iowa as sources of groundwater.

The Geological Survey Bureau initiated a study of these various river deposits in western Iowa during the late 1980's in an effort to understand their distribution, composition, origin, and water-bearing characteristics. Two general types were described: 1) sediments derived from glaciers or glacial deposits to the north and northeast, and 2) sediments resembling those in the modern Missouri and Platte rivers of Nebraska. Included in this latter group are fine-grained sediments called "salt and pepper" sands by well drillers in western Iowa. These sands form a potentially significant source of groundwater across some upland areas where they are commonly buried beneath 50 to 300 feet of glacial deposits. Scattered within the white quartz-rich sand grains are dark "pepper" grains which are identified as fragments of volcanic glass.

The "salt and pepper" sands exposed in a Mills County quarry show angled patterns of cross-bedding which reflect shifting current directions in an ancient river system with headwaters in the Rocky Mountains. *Photo by Greg Ludvigson*

Excerpts from article by Brian J. Witzke
Adapted from Iowa Geology 1991, No.16, Iowa Dept. of Natural Resources

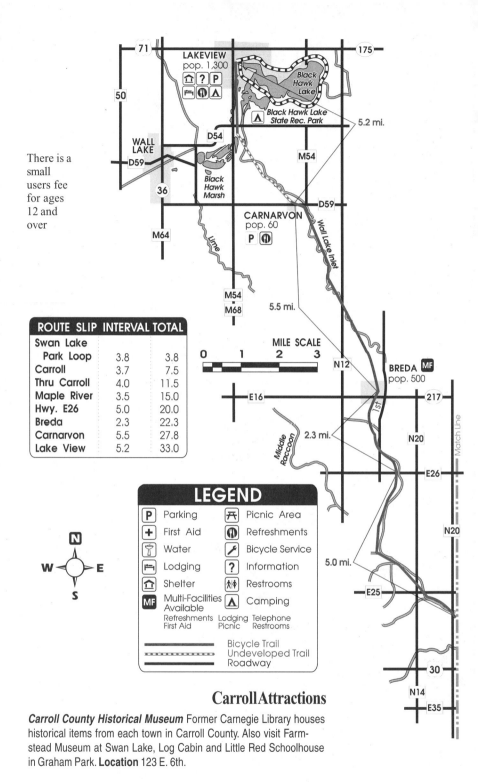

There is a small users fee for ages 12 and over

LAKEVIEW pop. 1,300

Black Hawk Lake

Black Hawk Lake State Rec. Park — 5.2 mi.

WALL LAKE

Black Hawk Marsh

CARNARVON pop. 60

5.5 mi.

2.3 mi.

BREDA MF pop. 500

5.0 mi.

Match Line

ROUTE SLIP	INTERVAL	TOTAL
Swan Lake Park Loop	3.8	3.8
Carroll	3.7	7.5
Thru Carroll	4.0	11.5
Maple River	3.5	15.0
Hwy. E26	5.0	20.0
Breda	2.3	22.3
Carnarvon	5.5	27.8
Lake View	5.2	33.0

MILE SCALE

0   1   2   3

N
W ← ✦ → E
S

LEGEND

P	Parking	⌇	Picnic Area
+	First Aid	🍴	Refreshments
⌇	Water	🔧	Bicycle Service
⌇	Lodging	?	Information
⌂	Shelter	🚻	Restrooms
MF	Multi-Facilities Available	⛺	Camping

Refreshments Lodging Telephone
First Aid Picnic Restrooms

━━━━━━ Bicycle Trail
┅┅┅┅┅ Undeveloped Trail
━━━━━━ Roadway

CarrollAttractions

Carroll County Historical Museum Former Carnegie Library houses historical items from each town in Carroll County. Also visit Farmstead Museum at Swan Lake, Log Cabin and Little Red Schoolhouse in Graham Park. **Location** 123 E. 6th.

Sauk Rail Trail — Swan Lake Park

Sauk Rail Trail
Swan Lake Park

Trail Length & Surface	Total Miles	Limestone Asphalt	Screening	Concrete	Developed
	33	3.8	13	1.5	14.7

Uses Leisure bicycling, cross-country skiing, in-line skating, hiking. *Equestrian use allowed adjacent to trail.*

Location & Setting West central Iowa between Carroll and Lakeview. Built on abandoned Chicago Northwestern rail bed for 13 miles and a 50 foot right-of-way for 20 miles. The area consists of prairies, wetlands, farmland and woodlands.

Information Carroll County Conservation Board (712) 792-4614
RR 1 Box 240A
Carron, IA 51401

Sac County Conservation Board (712) 662-4530
2970 280th Street
Sac City, IA 50583

County Carroll, Sac

Points of Interest

Swan Lake State Park Located 2.5 miles east of Carroll. A 510 acre multi-use area including bike and boat rentals, swimming, camping, picnicking, cross country skiing and snowmobiling.

SWAN LAKE PARK

Swan Lake

Sauk Rail Trail

To Hwy. 71
2 mi.

Wetland & Marsh

Bike Rentals Available

Loop = 3.8 mi.

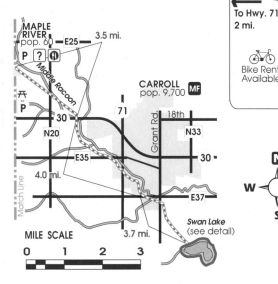

MAPLE RIVER pop. 60 E25 3.5 mi.

Middle Racoon

CARROLL pop. 9,700 MF

71
30
18th
N20
N33
E35
30
4.0 mi.
E37

Grant Rd.

Match Line

Swan Lake (see detail)

MILE SCALE

0   1   2   3

3.7 mi.

Points of Interest
ALONG THE TRAIL

Black Hawk Lake State Park
Black Hawk Marsh
Breda's Railroad Depot
Hazelbrush Wildlife Area
Mid-Prairie Park
Rolling Hills City Park, Carroll
Swan Lake State Park

Sioux City Area Trails

Location & Setting	Sioux City is located in northwest Iowa bordering both Nebraska and South Dakota across the Missouri River to the west.
Information	Siouxland Interstate Metropolitan Planning Council 400 Orpheum Electric Building Sioux City, IA 51102 (712) 279-6286
County	Woodbury

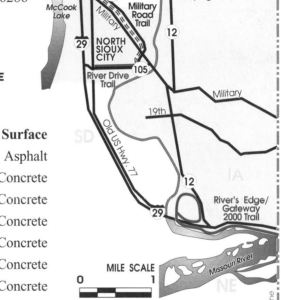

Trail Name	Length	Surface
Floyd River Trail	4.3	Asphalt
Chris Larson Trail	1.9	Concrete
Crystal Cove Trail	1.7	Concrete
River Drive	1.5	Concrete
39th Street Trail	1.0	Concrete
River's Edge Trail	3.3	Concrete
Chautauqua Park	3.0	Concrete
Singing Hills Trail	2.0	Concrete
Total	**18.7**	

Sioux City Attractions

Sergeant Floyd Riverboat Museum and Welcome Center Diesel inspection ship plied the Missouri River for 50 years as the flagship of the U.S. Army Corps of Engineers construction fleet. See the history of Missouri River transportation through rare photos, artifacts, dioramas and America's largest display of scale Missouri River steamboat and keelboat models, and Iowa's only professional model ship building shop. Special focus on the 1804 Lewis & Clark Expedition. **Location** 1000 Larson Park Rd. / Exit 149 on I-29.

Sioux City, Public Museum Built from pink colored Sioux Falls quartzite in the early 1890's, the Pierce mansion exhibits pioneer materials from antique needlework to a finished log cabin interior. Explore the natural history of the area through displays of birds, fish, animals and minerals. Indian artifacts displayed. **Location** 2901 Jackson St.

SHRA Railroad Museum Traces the history of the area's railroad industry. Photos, artifacts, large HO-scale model. Tours of railroad caboose and 1943 locomotive. Gift shop with railroad merchandise. **Location** 2001 Leech Ave.

Sioux City Art Center Traditional and contemporary art, permanent and traveling exhibits. Changing exhibits of contemporary Upper Midwest artwork. **Location** 513 Nebraska St.

FOREST CITY METEORITE Late in the afternoon of May 2, 1890, a meteorite sounding like heavy cannon fire, throwing off sparks, and trailing black smoke exploded about 11 miles northwest of Forest City in Winnebago County. The fall was observed from Sioux City to Grinnell and Mason City, and as far away as Chamberlain, South Dakota, 300 miles from the Winnebago County impact site. Rock fragments showered an eight square-mile area, and local residents reported a smell of sulphur. As with Iowa's other meteorites, fragments now are widely distributed in museums and private collections.

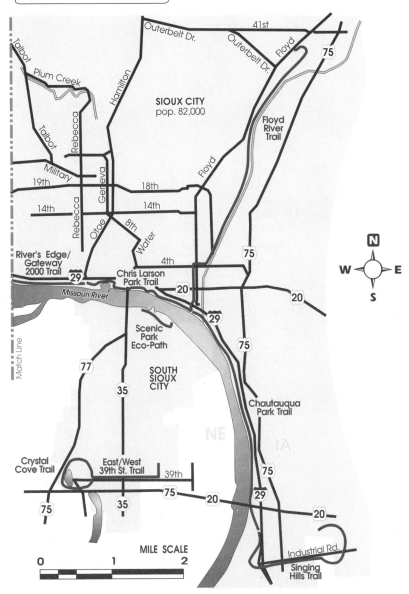

LEGEND

Bicycle Trail
Planned Trail
Roadway

Sioux City Area Trails

Stone State Park

Trail Length	10.0 miles (5 miles open to bicycling)
Surface	Natural
Uses	Fat tire bicycling, cross-country skiing, hiking, horseback riding, snowmobiling.
Location & Setting	Located in the northwest corner of Sioux City with 1,085 acres in Woodbury and Plymouth Counties. The Park can be accessed from Talbot Road off Memorial Drive.
Information	Stone State Park (712) 255-4698 Sioux City, IA 51103
County	Woodbury, Plymouth

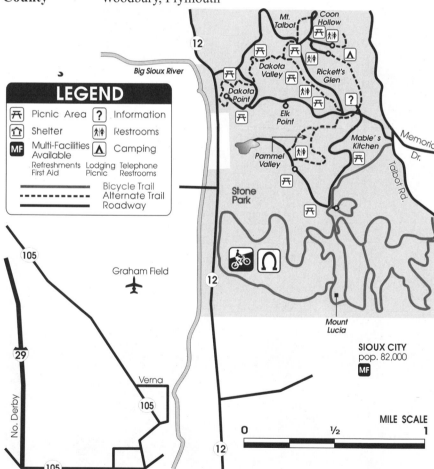

In addition to the trail system, park facilities include a lodge, and camping and picnic area. Stone Park is located entirely in the unique Loess Hills of western Iowa. These hills were formed many thousands of years ago by windblown soil.

Storm Lake's LakeTrail

Trail Length	5.0 miles
Surface	Concrete, plus sidewalks and low traffic streets.
Uses	Leisure bicycling, cross-country skiing, in-line skating, jogging
Location & Setting	Storm Lake in northwestern Iowa. The trail follows the north side of Storm Lake connecting the village of Lakeside at the east end with Emerald Park at the west end.
Information	Storm Lake Parks and Recreation Dept. (712) 732-8027
	620 Erie Street
	Storm Lake, IA 50588
County	Buena Vista

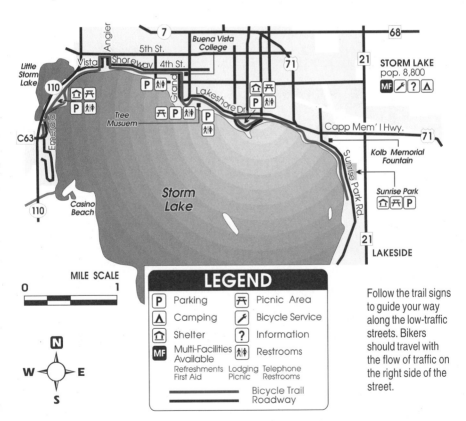

LEGEND

P	Parking	🎋	Picnic Area
A	Camping	🔧	Bicycle Service
⌂	Shelter	?	Information
MF	Multi-Facilities Available	🚻	Restrooms

Refreshments Lodging Telephone
First Aid Picnic Restrooms

━━━━━ Bicycle Trail
━━━━━ Roadway

Follow the trail signs to guide your way along the low-traffic streets. Bikers should travel with the flow of traffic on the right side of the street.

The five-mile trail links pathways, sidewalks and low-traffic streets and runs through recreation, historic and residential areas. Facilities at the parks include picnic areas, water sports and playgrounds.

COUNCIL BLUFFS

William Clark and Merriwether Lewis were searching for a northwest passage in 1804, when they met for a council with the Otoe and Missouri Indians on a bluff overlooking the Missouri River, hence the name "Council Bluffs".

ROUTE SLIP	INTERVAL	TOTAL
Council Bluffs		
Mineola	10.0	10.0
Silver City	4.5	14.5
Malvern	8.5	23.0
Imogene	13.5	36.5
Shenandoah	8.5	45.0
Izaak Walton Lodge	5.0	50.0
Coin	7.5	57.5
Blanchard	5.5	63.0

Points of Interest Include:

Bellevue, NE	Fontenelle Forest Nature Center
Council Bluffs	Lewis & Clark Monument
	General Dodge House
	Squirrel Cage Jail
Honey Creek	Hitchcock Nature Center
Malvern	Railroad Depot
Omaha, NE	Western Heritage Museum
Shenandoah	Restored Wabash Depot

Information	Iowa Natural Heritage Foundation 505 Fifth Avenue, Suite 444 Des Moines, IA 50309-2321	(515) 288-1846
	Council Bluffs Visitors Bureau 119 South Main Council Bluffs, IA 51501	(712) 325-1000
	Shenandoah Chamber of Commerce 403 West Sheridan Shenadoah, IA 51601	(712) 246-3260
County	Pottawattamie, Mills, Fremont, Page	

Wabash Trace Nature Trail

Wabash Trace Nature Trail

Trail Length	63.0 miles
Surface	Limestone screenings
Uses	Leisure bicycling, cross country skiing, hiking. *Equestrian use is permitted on a parallel trail on the northern five miles.*
Location & Setting	The Wabash Trace, located in southwest Iowa, is built on an abandoned rail bed and runs from Council Bluffs to Blanchard at the Missouri state line. The trail is frequently lined with trees that form beautiful tunnels. At the southern end of the trail, there are areas of prairie grasses which served as food for the herds of buffalo and deer that once roamed there. The Wabash Trace is a sanctuary for deer, rabbits, squirrels, wild turkeys, pheasants, quail and score of migratory birds and other animals.

Waubonsie State Park

Trail Length	8.0 miles
Surface	Natural
Uses	Fat tire bicycling, hiking, horseback riding, snowmobiling
Location & Setting	Southwest corner of the state, near the Missouri River. Sidney is 6 miles north and Hamburg is 9 miles south of the park.
Information	Waubonsie State Park (712) 382-2786 Rural Route 2, Box 66 Hamburg, IA 51640
County	Fremont

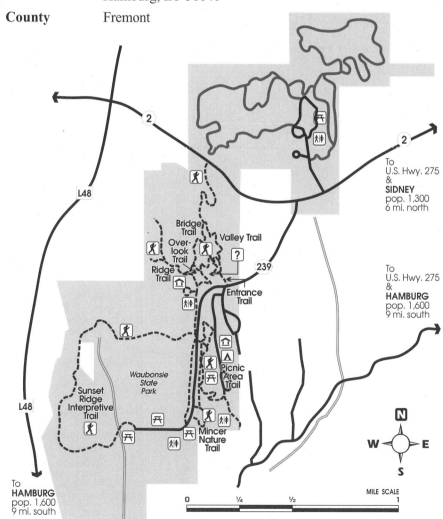

LEGEND

⛩ Picnic Area
🏠 Shelter
? Information
🚻 Restrooms
⛺ Camping

━━━ Bicycle Trail
----- Alternate
━━━ Roadway

Sidney Attractions

Fremont County Historical Museum Complex Multiple-building complex features Indian Room, mastodon tusks, kitchen, living room, bedroom, general store, old drug store fountain from 1863 Penn Drug, toys, clothes, farming equipment, genealogy records. **Location** East side of square.

The park is named for Chief Waubonsie of the Pottawattamie Indian tribe. With its steep ridges and scenic overlooks, visitors can see hills 50 miles away, and view four states: Nebraska, Iowa, Kansas and Missouri, as well as the Missouri River.

Waubonsie is located in the unique "Loess Hills", a landform found only along the Missouri River in Iowa and Missouri and in China. The unique topography of the park resembles the "badlands" of the west and harbors plants like the yucca which are normally found in more arid climates.

Waubonsie State Park

ROAD RELATED SYMBOLS

45 Interstate Highway
45 U.S. Highway
45 State Highway
45 County Highway

TRAIL USES

 Mountain Biking

 Leisure Biking

 In Line Skating

 (X-C) Cross-Country Skiing

 Hiking

 Horseback Riding

 Snowmobiling

AREA DESCRIPTIONS

 Parks, Schools, Preserves, etc.

 Waterway

 Mileage Scale

W-⊕-E Directional

FACILITIES

🔧 Bike Repair

⛺ Camping

➕ First Aid

? Info

🛏 Lodging

P Parking

⛩ Picnic

🍴 Refreshments

🚻 Restrooms

🏠 Shelter

🚰 Water

MF Multi Facilities Available

Refreshments   First Aid
Telephone   Picnic
Restrooms   Lodging

Western Iowa

Additional Trails — Non-Illustrated

Horseshoe Bend

Trail Length	3.5 miles
Surface	Natural-groomed
Uses	Fat tire bicycling, cross country skiing, hiking, horseback riding, snowmobiling.
Location & Setting	Located along the Little Sioux River 3.5 miles southwest of Milford in Dickinson County. Setting varies from hilly to flat.
Information	Dickinson County Conservation Board (712) 338-4786

Puddle Jumper Trail

Trail Length	2.3 miles
Surface	Crushed rock
Uses	Leisure bicycling, cross country skiing, hiking, snowmobiling.
Location & Setting	Sioux County between Orange City and Alton. Setting is open spaces, prairie, farmland.
Information	Orange City (City Hall) (712) 737-4885

Rock Rapids Trail

Trail Length	1.0 mile
Surface	Asphalt
Uses	Leisure bicycling, in-line skating
Location & Setting	Rock Rapids, from the town bridge across the Rock River forming a loops around the community center.
Information	Rock Rapids (712) 472-2511

Spencer Recreation Trail

Trail Length	1.5 miles (4.5 miles planned)
Surface	Concrete, crushed limestone
Uses	Leisure bicycling, in-line skating, jogging
Location & Setting	City of Spencer in Clay County. The trail travels around a pond in Stolley Park and along the Little Sioux River. The setting is wooded lowland and gently rolling landscape. The trail currently ends at rail tracks west of the pond, but will extend to East Leach Park and Oneota Park.
Information	Spencer Park Dept. (712) 264-7260

Upper Nish Habitat Trail

Trail Length	6.0 miles
Surface	Ballast, dirt
Uses	Fat tire bicycling, hiking
Location & Setting	Located east of Irwin in Shelby County on former railroad right-of-way.
Information	Shelby County Conservation Board (712) 755-2628

Winkel Memorial Trail

Trail Length	6.0 miles
Surface	Natural-groomed
Uses	Fat tire bicycling, cross country skiing, hiking, horseback riding, snowmobiling.
Location & Setting	Osceola County. Sibley to Allendorf with a spur to Willow Creek County Recreation Area. Former railroad right-of-way. The Sibley public golf course is adjacent to a portion of the trail.
Information	Osceola County Conservation Board (712) 758-3709

Central Iowa Bike Route

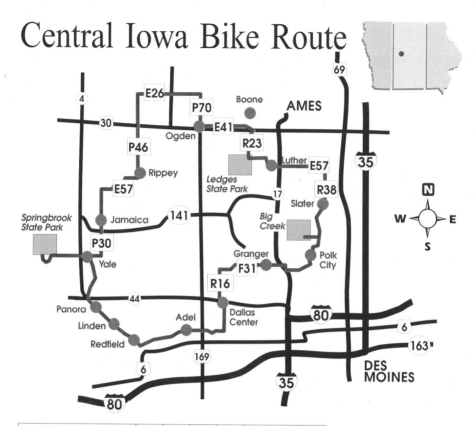

Facilities & Service Available	Restrooms	Food	Restaurants	Drinking Water	Camping	Lodging	Gear Shuttle
Big Creek State Park	X	X		X			X
Slater	X	X	X	X			
Luther	X	X		X			
Ledges State Park	X			X	X		
Boone	X	X	X	X	X	X	X
Ogden	X	X	X	X			
Rippey	X	X		X			
Jamaica	X	X		X			
Yale	X	X		X			
Springbrook State Park	X	X	X				
Panora	X	X	X	X		X	
Linden	X			X			
Redfield	X			X			
Adel	X	X	X	X		X	
Dallas Center	X	X	X	X			X
Granger	X	X		X			
Polk City	X	X	X	X			
Big Creek State Park	X	X		X			X

It is not necessary to ride State Highway 210 to reach Slater. At the intersection of R38 and Highway 210, proceed north .3 miles on gravel. Turn east and ride .5 miles adjacent to the railroad tracks.

The Central Iowa Bike Route

connects Big Creek, Ledges and Springbrook State Parks as it ambles through 14 charming towns, both large and small. The route is relatively flat, with a few challenging hills as you make your way across the picturesque valleys of the Des Moines and Raccoon Rivers.

You may ride the paved Raccoon Valley Trail between Yale and just west of Adel. A daily trail pass is required and can be purchased at the trailhead.

Mileage

Big Creek State Park	4	14	27	35	45	51	57	63	69	75	82	93	118	128	134	139	152	160
Polk City		10	23	31	41	47	53	59	65	71	78	89	114	124	130	135	148	156
Granger			13	21	31	37	43	49	55	61	68	79	104	114	120	125	138	146
Dallas Center				8	18	24	30	36	42	48	55	66	91	101	107	112	125	133
Adel					10	16	22	28	34	40	47	58	83	93	99	104	117	125
Redfield						6	12	18	24	30	37	48	73	83	89	94	107	115
Linden							6	12	18	24	31	42	67	77	83	88	101	109
Panora								6	12	18	25	36	61	71	77	82	95	103
Yale									6	12	19	30	55	65	71	76	89	97
Springbrook State Park										6	13	24	49	59	65	70	83	91
Yale											7	18	43	53	59	64	77	85
Jamaica												11	36	46	52	57	70	78
Rippey													25	35	41	46	59	67
Ogden														10	16	21	34	42
Boone															6	11	24	32
Ledges State Park																5	18	26
Luther																	13	21
Slater																		8
Big Creek State Park																		

Mileage shown illustrates the Central State Park Bike Route, which is a 160 mile ride in its entirety, starting at Big Creek State Park and ending at Big Creek State Park. Route maybe ridden in either direction.

Ledges State Park Serviceberry

Ken Formanek

Photo Courtesy of Iowa Dept. of Natural Resources

Detailed directions for the route between Granger and Polk City or Big Creek:

Ride east of Granger on F31 (2.5 miles); turn left or north on NW121 (2 miles) at Golf Course Road. Turn right on NW118 which becomes N. Beaver Dr., which becomes NW107; at the T, turn left on 106 for .5 miles; turn left at the cemetery onto 112th and travel across the mile long bridge over Saylorville Lake. After the bridge, you may either take the bike trail to Big Creek or continue on the road to Polk City. To reach Big Creek State Park, ride .25 miles after the bridge. On the right side of the road there is a paved parking lot at the trail access. This trail takes you to Big Creek.

Central Iowa Bike Route

Lake to Lake Bike Route

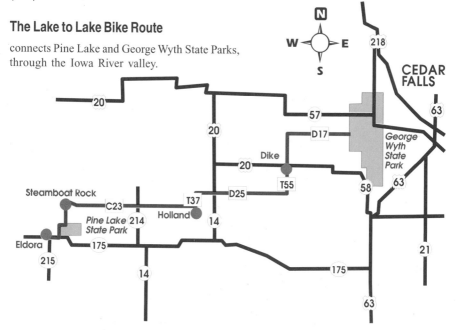

There are 25 miles of surfaced bike trails within the Cedar Falls/ Waterloo metropolitan area and more are planned for completion in the future.

The trail head for the 52 mile Cedar Valley Nature Trail, which connects Cedar Falls/ Waterloo with Cedar Rapids, is located on the southeast edge of Waterloo.

Trail passes are required for users age 11 and older.

Black Hawk County Conservation Board
(319) 266-6813

The Lake to Lake Bike Route

connects Pine Lake and George Wyth State Parks, through the Iowa River valley.

Cold weather shouldn't stop the avid biker. Newly renovated cabins at Pine Lake are open year-round.

Photo Courtesy of Iowa Dept. of Natural Resources

Ken Formanek

Facilities & Service Available	Restrooms	Food	Restaurants	Drinking Water	Camping	Lodging	Gear Shuttle
George Wyth State Park	X	X		X	X		X
Cedar Falls/Waterloo	X	X	X	X		X	X
Dike	X	X	X	X			
Holland	X		X	X			
Steamboat Rock	X	X		X			
Pine Lake State Park	X			X	X		X
Eldora	X	X	X	X		X	

Mileage shown illustrates the Lake-to-Lake bike route, which is a 50 mile ride in its entirety, starting at George Wyth State Park and ending at Pine Lake State Park. Route may be ridden in either direction.

Mileage

George Wyth State Park	7	18	31	45	49	50
Cedar Falls/Waterloo		11	24	38	42	43
Dike			13	27	31	32
Holland				14	18	19
Steamboat Rock					4	5
Pine Lake State Park						1
Eldora						

GEAR SHUTTLE SERVICE

Some bed and breakfasts, motels and park concessionaires offer shuttle service for gear or luggage at a nominal fee. Reservations for this service must be made in advance and some require a minimum number of persons.

OVERNIGHT VEHICLE PARKING

Arrangements must be made in advance to leave your vehicle overnight in any of Iowa's state parks. Park rangers will direct you to the lot designated for over night parking, generally a visitor parking lot adjacent to the campground.

Route Clarifications:

Holland to Dike: You must back track .5 mile north on Hwy. T37.

Dike to George Wyth State Park through Cedar Falls: Co. Hwy. D17 becomes 27th St.; turn right (or south) on Hudson Rd.; follow Hudson Road to the beginning of Hudson Road Bike Trail which leads to the Green Hill Bike Trail; turn left or east and follow the Green Hill Bike Trail for approximately 6 miles until it crosses the Cedar River to George Wyth State Park; follow the signs to the campground.

Pine Lake State Park

Mark Edwards

Photo Courtesy of Iowa Dept. of Natural Resources

Lake to Lake Bike Route

North East Iowa Bike Route

The Great River Road has paved shoulders which were designed for bicycle traffic. It is a long winding road along the banks of the scenic and legendary Mississippi River.

Coast down and pedal up the steep hills. This route is designed for the "seasoned" cyclist.

Facilities & Service Available	Restrooms	Food	Restaurants	Drinking Water	Camping	Lodging	Gear Shuttle
Wapsipinicon State Park	X			X	X		
Anamosa	X	X	X	X		X	X
Prairieburg	X			X			
Delhi	X	X	X	X			
Manchester	X	X	X	X		X	
Dundee	X	X		X			
Backbone State Park	X			X	X		X
Petersburg	X	X	X	X			
Colesburg	X	X	X	X			
Osterdock	X	X	X	X			
Guttenburg	X	X	X	X		X	
Pikes Peak State Park	X			X	X		
McGregor	X	X	X	X		X	X

The North East Iowa Bike Route

connects Wapsipinicon, Pikes Peak and Backbone State Parks. Popularly known as the "Little Switzerland" of Iowa, this route is marked by breathtaking bluffs tree topped hills, roller coaster roads and meandering rivers.

Mileage

Wapsipinicon State Park	19	39	48	60	64	68	66	93	101	108	124	130
Prairieburg		20	29	41	45	49	47	74	82	89	105	111
Delhi			9	21	25	29	47	54	62	69	85	91
Manchester				12	16	20	38	45	53	60	76	82
Dundee					4	8	26	33	41	48	64	70
Backbone State Park						4	22	29	37	44	60	66
Dundee							18	25	33	40	56	62
Petersburg								7	15	22	38	44
Colesburg									8	15	31	37
Osterdock										7	23	29
Guttenberg											16	22
Pikes Peak State Park												6
McGregor												

Mileage shown illustrates the Northeast Iowa bike route, which is a 130 mile ride in its entirety, starting at Wapsi-pinicon State Park and ending at McGregor. Route may be ridden in either direction.

Route Clarifications:

Anamosa: E28 can be found by going west of *Caseys* store on Cherry St.

Prairieburg to Delhi: West on E28/X20; north on X20; east on D62; north on X31.

Delhi to Manchester: Return to south edge of Delhi to take D5X.

Manchester: Will come into town on D5X (Bailey Drive); go west on Main St. which becomes D22.

Dundee to Petersburg: *NOTE* The route jogs on State Hwy. 38 for .2 mile.

Petersburg to Colesburg: *NOTE* The route jogs east on State Hwy. 3 for .4 mile just before Colesburg.

Guttenberg to Pikes Peak State Park: Take X56, the Great River Road, out of Guttenberg.

Pikes Peak State Park to McGregor: State Hwy. 340 does not have paved shoulders.

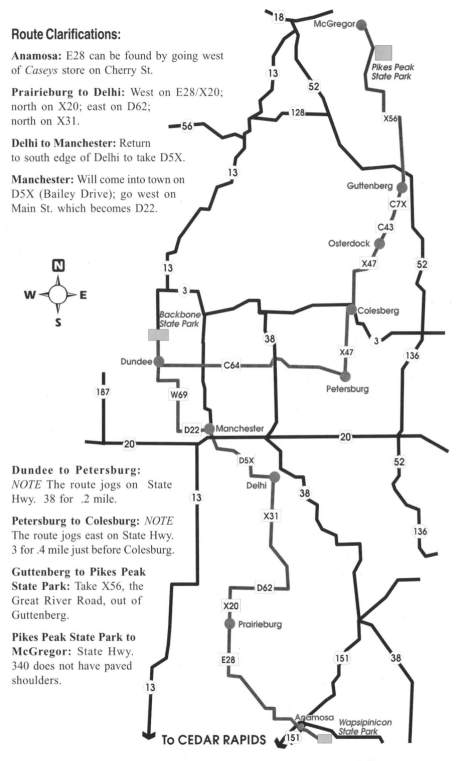

North East Iowa Bike Route

South East Iowa Bike Route

This route travels along State Highway 1 for .6 mile from Lacey-Keosauqua State Park to Highway J40. It is possible to ride on the wide gravel shoulder.

The South East Iowa Route

follows along a portion of the Woodland Scenic Byway. Share the roads with the horses and buggies of the Amish residents; enjoy architecture in the National Historic Districts of the villages of Bentonsport and Bonaparte; and in Keosauqua, visit Iowa's oldest county courthouse in continuous use as well as Pearson House, a station on the *"underground railroad."*

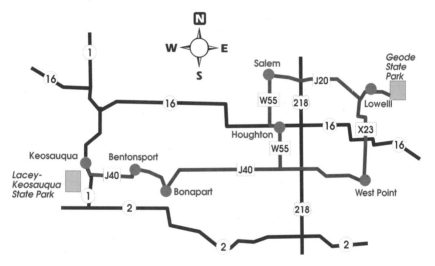

The Forest Craft Festival is held at Lacey-Keosauqua State Park the second weekend of October. It features wood craft demonstrations and sales, forest and wildlife management techniques and colorful buckskinners.

Facilities & Service Available	Restrooms	Food	Restaurants	Drinking Water	Camping	Lodging
Keosauqua	X	X	X	X		X
Keosauqua State Park	X			X	X	
Bentonsport	X	X		X		X
Bonaparte	X	X	X	X		X
Houghton	X	X		X		
Salem	X	X		X		
Lowell						
Geode State Park	X	X		X	X	
West Point	X	X	X	X		

There are many annual celebrations & festivals, including *Bike Van Buren,* held annually during the third weekend of Aug-ust. The two-day event draws more than 400 bicyclists.

Carry your gear and *rough it* in the campgrounds or take comfort in a local bed and breakfast or motel along the route.

Mileage

Origin	Bentonsport	Bonaparte	Houghton	Salem	Lowell	Geode State Park	Lowell	West Point	Bonaparte	Bentonsport	Keosauqua State Park
Keosauqua State Park	8	12	27	32	42	48	54	63	82	86	93
Bentonsport		4	19	24	34	40	46	55	74	78	85
Bonaparte			15	20	30	36	42	51	70	74	81
Houghton				5	15	21	27	36	55	59	66
Salem					10	16	22	31	50	54	61
Lowell						6	12	21	40	44	51
Geode State Park							6	15	34	38	46
Lowell								9	28	32	40
West Point									19	23	31
Bonaparte										4	12
Bentonsport											8
Keosauqua State Park											

Mileage shown illustrates the Southeast Iowa bike route, which is a 93 mile ride in its entirety, starting and ending at Lacey-Keosauqua State Park. Route may be ridden in either direction.

SAFETY TIPS

- The Lake-To-Lake Bike Route is mostly county highways. Ride on the right side of the road and obey all traffic laws. Be alert at intersections.

- Do not create a traffic jam. Ride in double or single file, as traffic dictates.

- Wear a helmet. Even a slow fall from a bicycle is enough to create serious injury.

- Wear bright colors while bicycling on roadways.

Pedal through scenic splendor

as you explore Iowa's state parks along four bicycle routes, developed to help you enjoy these "places of quiet beauty." Routes primarily travel paved county highways, with an occasional stretch of bicycle trail.

Christine Quinn

Lake Geode in the summer.

Photo Courtesy of Iowa Dept. of Natural Resources

Southeast Iowa Bike Route

County to Trail Index

City to Trail Index

City	Trail Name	Page

City to Trail Index (Continued)

City	Trail Name	Page

A Message from the Iowa Trails Council

Have you ever thought about how trails you enjoy came about? Someone first had to *conceive the idea*. Without that thought it would not have happened. After the idea is conceived there is a great deal of labor before the actual *birth* of a trail, with considerable expense involved in the endeavor.

We purchase expensive bicycles, jogging clothes and hiking shoes, skis, snowmobiles and gasoline to get to these trails. Sometimes we pay a fee to help with trail maintenance. Members of the Iowa Trails Council, by their membership, have contributed directly to the *birth and development* of hundreds of miles of trails.

Yes, trees do grow on Iowa's trails
but you know trails do not grow on trees.
Trails are conceived and nurtured by people;
people just like you and me.
No one can build and preserve a major trail all alone.
The ITC needs you and you need us.
Let's conceive and nurture trails in Iowa together.

The Iowa Trails Council is the *only* trails organization in Iowa devoted exclusively to the acquisition, development and promotion of trails. It is a not for profit organization composed of volunteers. Contributions are used **only** to create more and better trails and are tax deductible. The Trails Advocate magazine is sent to all members and subscribers.

The Trails State

**IOWA
TRAILS COUNCIL**

The Iowa Trails Council was founded in 1984. Today there are thousands of miles of trails in Iowa's parks and in metropolitan areas. Due largely to the efforts of the Council there are now more than 50 railroad rights-of-way converted in Iowa, amounting to more than 700 miles of rail trails!

Share in this effort by joining and supporting the ITC today.

I wish to contribute to Iowa Trails as a

___	Sponsoring Member	*MORE THAN* $100
___	Supporting Member	$100
___	Sustaining Member	$50
___	Contributing Member	$25
___	TA Subscriber only	$15

Name _____

Street _____

City _____

State ____ Zip _____ Tel.# _____

Mail to: **Iowa Trails Council**
Post Office Box 131
Center Point, IA 52213-0131
(319) 849-1844

To order additional copies of this book:

Pay by Check or Credit Card

Mail Check to:

American Bike Trails
1157 South Milwaukee Avenue
Libertyville, IL 60048

Book *(per copy)* $14.95
Handling *(per order)* $2.00
Sales Tax—IL residents *(per copy)* $1.00

To order by Credit Card call (800) 246-4627

American Bike Trails

published and distributes maps, books and guides

for the recreational bicyclist. Our trail maps

cover over 250 trails throughout the states of

Illinois, Iowa, Michigan, Minnesota and Wisconsin.

For a free copy of our catalog write to the above address